The Eight Ministries of the HOLY SPIRIT

From Denomination to Reformation:
An Introduction to Biblecostalism™

F. Josephus Johnson, II
Foreword by Pastor Jack Hayford

WINEPRESS WP PUBLISHING

© 2005 by Bishop Joey Johnson. All rights reserved.

Packaged by WinePress Publishing, PO Box 428, Enumclaw, WA 98022. The views expressed or implied in this work do not necessarily reflect those of WinePress Publishing. The author(s) is ultimately responsible for the design, content and editorial accuracy of this work.

No part of this publication may be reproduced, stored in a retrieval system or transmitted in any way by any means—electronic, mechanical, photocopy, recording or otherwise—without the prior permission of the copyright holder, except as provided by USA copyright law.

Unless otherwise noted scripture references are taken from the New American Standard Bible® copyright © 1960, 1962, 1963, 1968, 1971, 1972, 1973, 1975, 1977, 1995 by The Lockman Foundation. Used by permission.

Scripture quotations marked NLT are taken from the Holy Bible, New Living Translation, copyright 1996. Used by permission of Tyndale House Publishers, Inc., Wheaton, Illinois 60189. All rights reserved.

Scripture references marked KJV are taken from the King James Version of the Bible.

ISBN 1-57921-746-X
Library of Congress Catalog Card Number: 2004103497

Table of Contents

Preface

OUT OF THE CLOSET AND INTO THE SPOTLIGHT

In 1960, I accepted the Lord as my personal Savior through a dramatic experience. This was at the age of eight years old. In a little, dimly lit, Pentecostal Church, I received Jesus into my heart as Savior and Lord, and the Holy Spirit knocked me to the floor and rolled me all up under those chairs and pews, even though I had never heard of or seen such a thing.

That was the glorious beginning of what would turn out to be a very frustrating experience with Pentecostalism.

I use the term "Pentecostalism" to refer to those who hold to the doctrine of evidentiary tongues, i.e. that you must speak in tongues to be baptized in the Holy Ghost. I do not use the term pejoratively, but simply as a means of identifying a specific stream of belief or denomination.

The unique tributary of the particular stream that I grew up in did not overtly teach evidentiary tongues, but yet practiced a more extreme version of that teaching. They treated you as if you were unsaved, if you had not spoken in tongues—and if you had not spoken in tongues to their specific criteria and liking.

I later received the baptism in the Holy Spirit, because of badgering, abuse, and shame, but was **not** sure about what I had received or of its purpose.

I eventually acknowledged my call to the ministry and organized The House of The Lord on March 6, 1974. Because of the abuses that I had experienced in that tributary of Pentecostalism, which I would pejoratively characterize as "extreme Pentecostalism," I reacted against that teaching and everything connected with it. I heard Howard Hendricks say once, "Whenever you react, you are in danger of setting up an extreme." *Well, The House of the Lord, as blessed as it was of the Lord, was extreme in its early reaction to Pentecostalism.* We reacted into a form of "Evangelicalism" that was close to "extreme Fundamentalism." I used the term "Evangelicalism" to refer to those who give a prominent place to preaching the Evangel, i.e. the Gospel, and those who have a high allegiance to the inerrancy of the Word of God. They generally owe their theological perspectives to the "Fundamentalists." I used the term "Fundamentalism" to refer to those who were a part of the

"Fundamental" or back to the Bible movement of the early 1920s. The movement began as a legitimate reaction to liberal theology. I use the term "extreme Fundamentalists" to describe those of the "Fundamental" movement who became antimodernists and separatists who railed on fellow believers, with a harsh spirit, if they didn't agree with them in every detail of doctrine.

This spirit had impacted me and, consequently, our church in the early years of our existence. We were highly intellectual and had very little place for emotion and **no** place for the spiritual manifestations of 1 Corinthians 12:8–12—even though God worked through a few of them any way, from time to time. We were in a denominational box, particularly when it came to anything having to do with emotion or the manifestations of the Spirit.

Furthermore, I was hostile against those who spoke in tongues and vehemently opposed them. I looked at Pentecostals as mindless automatons who were merely reacting to their emotions and experiences with **no** biblical basis whatsoever.

This characterization of those who accepted any display of the spiritual manifestations of 1 Corinthians 12:8–10, was not mine alone, but was the evaluation of a group of Fundamentalists and Evangelicals called Cessationists, who believed that all spiritual manifestations—particularly those of 1 Corinthians 12:8–10—had permanently ceased with the passing of the last of the twelve apostles, along with the gifted positions of apostle and prophet.

From the 1920s to the 1970s, Cessationists wielded a considerable amount of power and influence. This power and influence was used not only to propagate the doctrine of cessationism, but to pummel and persecute anyone who would dare hold an opposite position. This caused both the Pentecostals and the Charismatics, i.e. the Neo-Pentecostal movement that penetrated the historical denominations of the 60s and 70s (*They did not necessarily teach evidentiary tongues*), to carry around with them a low-grade shame for believing what they believed. This pummelling left many Pentecostals and Charismatics feeling like abused stepchildren.

It was in this context, resting in a box or closet of denominationalism, that God began to call me to restudy the ministry of the Holy Spirit in Acts 2, 8, 10, 19, and 1 Corinthians 12–14.

I unofficially started this process through a message preached for our "Logos Bible Institute" Chapel service, on Monday, December 27, 1993, with a message entitled, "Where's the Beef?" That question was taken from a series of then famous Wendy's commercials, and the message was based on Acts 1:8. The entire question of the message was, "If we are supposed to have power after the Holy Spirit has come upon us to be effective witnesses of the Gospel of Jesus Christ and transact Kingdom business in that power . . . Where's the beef?"

I officially started the process in our church, i.e. The House of the Lord, in Akron, Ohio, on October 1, 1997, with a series entitled: "The Tongues Trilemma." I chose this title, because the debate between Evangelicals and Pentecostals posed the problem and question in terms of a dilemma, or a choice between two options. Nevertheless, I was putting forth a third option.

Well, this immediately plunged me into a transitional period of great persecution, misunderstanding, and *a dark night of the soul*, even though God continued to bless our evangelism, attendance, offerings, and building projects.

Seven years later, hundreds of sermons later, any number of members and leaders later, after much pain, intense study, intense seeking the Lord, moving into the manifestations of the Lord, and great spiritual blessings, *I believe God is calling me out of the closet and into the spotlight!!!*

The closet is a place of retreat and privacy. That is where I preferred to stay. Now, please don't misunderstand me. I had some aspirations as a young Evangelical preacher with a growing church and a growing reputation for an ability to exegete, teach, and preach the Word of God. But, when God changed my theological orientation, I would have much preferred to stay in the closet . . . in the shadows. That would also be closer to my temperament.

Nevertheless, my life is not my own and I believe I heard God calling me to come out of the closet of retreat and to come into the spotlight. The spotlight is the place of conspicuous attention. The attention is conspicuous, because it seems to be a violation of good taste, good sense, or in my case "good" or sound doctrine. Yet, this is not something that I have voluntarily chosen, but something that I feel called to do. I am compelled to teach and preach a wider, biblical perspective of things that neither totally refutes the Pentecostals nor totally rails against the Evangelicals—and woe is me if I don't heed God's call.

I wish that I could tell you my whole story, but that will have to await another work. *Let it suffice to say that God is doing a new thing, not just in our church, but around the world!* We are **not** *classically* Pentecostal, we are Biblecostal™. *The heart of this doctrine is that I accept the Evangelical perspective of the person and work of the Holy Spirit, but I also believe that the baptism in the Holy Spirit is an experience that is subsequent to (or after) salvation, potentially available to all believers, for power for calling, service, ministry vocation, praise, worship, and spiritual warfare, and each occurrence of this experience in Luke–Acts is accompanied by inspired speech (whether that is inspired English or tongues), and that inspired speech tends to be tongues and/or prophecy.* Before you put the book down, please give me a chance to prove that biblically.

We are a part of the new wineskin that God is developing to receive the new wine of the Holy Spirit that He is pouring out in anticipation of the final manifestation of His Kingdom.

I am reminded of what Peter wrote:

But you are a chosen race, a royal priesthood, a holy nation, a people for God's own possession, so that you may proclaim the excellencies of Him who has called you out of darkness into His marvelous light.

(1 Peter 2:9)

This verse is about Israelites who had become a part of the Church of Jesus Christ, but I want to apply it to me, our church, and thousands of other churches in this country and many oversees. It is time for us to come out of darkness, out of the closet, out of shame, and into the marvelous light of the glorious Gospel of Jesus Christ and the heretofore uncharted frontier of the revelation of biblical teaching, study, and knowledge concerning the baptism in the Holy Ghost. Although I had always thought of Pentecostalism and anything Charismatic as nothing more than emotional froth on the top of a root beer, I can now see a clear biblical basis for a credible belief in more than the conservative Evangelical perspective of the Holy Spirit and His ministry—even if I don't go as far as some extreme Pentecostals.

Clark Pinnock, quoted in *The Charismatic Theology of St. Luke*, written by Roger Strondstad, states that "If canonical Luke has a charismatic theology as Stronstad proves, we cannot consider Pentecostalism to be a kind of aberration born of experiential excesses, but a twentieth century revival of New Testament theology and religion."[1] Stronstad uses the term "charismatic" to "mean God's gift of His Spirit

---

[1] Roger Stronstad, *The Charismatic Theology of St. Luke*, Hendrickson Publishers, Inc., Peabody Massachusetts, 1984, vii-viii.

to His servants, either individually or collectively, to anoint, empower, or inspire them for divine service. As it is recorded in the Scripture, therefore, this charismatic activity is necessarily an experiential phenomenon."[2]

Incidentally, if you want a book that puts forth what I believe, in a thorough and scholarly way, it would be that book: *The Charismatic Theology of St. Luke*, written by Roger Strondstad. His book, along with the life and ministry of Pastor Jack Hayford, have had a profound impact upon my theology. I thank them for their lives and teaching, but any views in this book ultimately remain mine.

With respect to the debate between Evangelicals and Pentecostals, Stronstad said "This division is not simply theological. Fundamental hermeneutical or methodological differences lie at the heart of the matter."[3] *In other words, the division is not simply concerning the study of religion, there are basic or central interpretive or methodological differences in handling the text that lie at the heart of the division.*

The difference emerges out of the different kinds of literary genre that are used in the New Testament. The Gospel of Luke and the book of Acts are basically narrative history of the founding and growth of Christianity, whereas Paul's writings are addressed to some particular

---

[2] Roger Stronstad, *The Charismatic Theology Of St. Luke*, Hendrickson Publishers, Inc., Peabody Massachusetts, 1984, 13.
[3] Roger Stronstad, *The Charismatic Theology Of St. Luke*, Hendrickson Publishers, Inc., Peabody Massachusetts, 1984, 2.

circumstance and are pastoral. Therein lies a major part of the problem. Evangelicals advocate a method of interpretation that drives a wedge between narrative and teaching, between history and theology. Noted Evangelical scholar, John R. Stott, wrote in his widely influential book, *The Baptism and Fullness of the Holy Spirit*, "This revelation of the purpose of God in Scripture should be sought in *didactic (teaching)*, rather than its *historical* parts. More precisely, we should look for it in the teaching of Jesus, and in the sermons and writings of the apostles, and not in the purely narrative portions of Acts."[4] Later in the same book Stott reiterates, "A doctrine of the Holy Spirit must not be constructed from descriptive passages in Acts."[5] *This position by Stott has become axiomatic among Evangelicals.*

If we are going to be able to come out of the closet and into the spotlight, there are three problems that must be resolved, according to Stronstad: "1) the literary and theological homogeneity (*or uniformity*) of Luke-Acts, 2) the theological character of the Lukan historiography (*or history of Luke*), and 3) the independence of Luke as a theologian."[6]

---

[4] John R. W. Stott, *The Baptism and Fullness of the Holy Spirit*, 8. This book went through eight American printings before it was issued as an expanded second edition in 1975.
[5] John R. W. Stott, *The Baptism and Fullness of the Holy Spirit*, 18.
[6] Roger Stronstad, *The Charismatic Theology of St. Luke*, Hendrickson Publishers, Inc., Peabody Massachusetts, 1984, 2.

So, let me briefly address these three problems, before we dive into the meat of the book.

1. Problem #1: The Literary and Theological Uniformity of Luke-Acts.

   Interpreters often treat Luke and Acts as if there is a discontinuity between them, but there is no serious challenge to the scholarly consensus that the Gospel of Luke and the book of Acts are two parts of one literary unit. Once this is acknowledged, we can then began to work on a Lukan doctrine of the Holy Spirit, and that doctrine is based upon Luke's view of the Holy Spirit in both books. I am not saying there are absolutely no differences between the way that Luke sees the Holy Spirit in the Gospel and the book of Acts, because the Holy Spirit's ministry still seems to be largely individual in Luke, but potentially universal in the book of Acts. Nevertheless, the essential character of the ministry of the Holy Spirit remains the same in both books.

   This realization will allow us to study the use of the same terms, by the same writer, and see the continuity between terms like "filled with the Spirit" in both Luke and Acts.

2. Problem #2: The Theological Character of the History of Luke.

I have already mentioned the fact that many Evangelicals believe that narrative text cannot be used to determine doctrines or normative patterns of behavior. *Yet, the distinction between narrative and teaching is alien to biblical historiography.* Paul himself saw a teaching purpose in historical narrative. He wrote:

> All Scripture is inspired by God and profitable for teaching, for reproof, for correction, for training in righteousness; so that the man of God may be adequate, equipped for every good work.
>
> (2 Timothy 3:16–17)

Paul did **not** say *some* Scripture was inspired for teaching or all Scripture *except* for narrative portions, but *all* Scripture is God-breathed and profitable for teaching.

Paul also wrote:

> For whatever was written in earlier times was written for our instruction, so that through perseverance and the encouragement of the Scriptures we might have hope.
>
> (Romans 15:4)

This undoubtedly refers to the Old Testament.

Furthermore, in 1 Corinthians Paul, referring to the experience of Israel in the wilderness, said in:

> Now these things happened to them as an example, and they were written for our instruction, upon whom the ends of the ages have come.
>
> (1 Corinthians 10:11)

Stronstad remarks, "If for Paul the historical narratives of the Old Testament had didactic lessons for New Testament Christians, then it would be most surprising if Luke, who modelled his historiography after the Old Testament historiography, did not invest his own history of the origin and spread of Christianity with a *didactic (i.e. teaching)* significance."[7]

This is particularly important because the historical narratives of the Old Testament served as a model for Luke's historiography. Luke did not model his writings after the Hellenistic writings of his time, but the Old Testament, and they are frequently reminiscent of the Septuagint (*i.e. the Greek translation of the Old Testament*). "The Septuagint Greek version of the Old Testament is one of the most important and the most an-

---

[7] Roger Stronstad, *The Charismatic Theology of St. Luke*, Hendrickson Publishers, Inc., Peabody Massachusetts, 1984, 7.

cient of all the versions. According to tradition, 72 Jewish scholars completed it. In fact, the word *Septuagint* means 'seventy.' It was completed in Alexandria about 285 B.C., a time when more was known of Hebrew than any time since . . . Almost every quotation of the Old Testament that is found in the New Testament is an exact reproduction of the Septuagint reading."[8] So, in addition to the writings of Luke, the Bible is a Hebrew book—not a Greek book.

By now you may be thinking, "So what?" Well, Luke's deliberate choice of modelling his writings after the Septuagint, as opposed to the Hellenistic tradition, demonstrates that Luke is not just an historian, but a theologian. Luke was writing from both a historical and theological perspective.

The fact that Luke was a historian was put forth in a book that changed the theological landscape, when I. Howard Marshall wrote: *Luke: Historian and Theologian*. With this revelation, a new view became easier to adopt. We no longer have to view Luke as merely an historian, whose history has little or no impact upon theology. We can now view him as a theologian whose view of theology led him to write an important history.

---

[8] James T. Davis, *Redefining the Role of Women in the Church*, Christian International Ministries Network, Santa Rosa Beach, Florida, 37–38.

Furthermore, we can begin to challenge the notion that history and theology or narratives and doctrine stand in opposition to one another.

In the light of these revelations, Stronstad proposes that the actual nature of the Lukan narratives is "1) episodic, 2) typological, 3) programmatic, and/or 4) paradigmatic."[9]

- The narratives are episodic or they deal with specific episodes.
- The narratives are typological and look to the Old Testament for episodes that prophesy the events in Luke and Acts. For instance the transfer of the Holy Spirit from Jesus Christ to the Church, through the events of Acts 2, find their antitypes in the transfers of Moses to the Seventy and Elijah to Elisha.
- The narratives are also programmatic, i.e. they point towards the unfolding of future events. And finally,
- The narratives are paradigmatic. A paradigmatic narrative is one that has normative features for the mission and

---

[9] Roger Stronstad, *The Charismatic Theology of St. Luke*, Hendrickson Publishers, Inc., Peabody Massachusetts, 1984, 8.

character of God's people living in the last days.[10]

Therefore, we have firm historical and theological accounts upon which to establish a "Lukan" doctrine of the Holy Spirit which has normative implications for the mission and religious experience of the contemporary Church.[11]

3. Problem #3: The Independence of Luke As a Theologian.
    The tendency to treat historical narrative and teaching as totally separate and almost irreconcilable has led to the widespread belief that we look to Luke for history and to Paul for theology. Therefore, Luke's history is interpreted as though it was written by Paul.

    So, Luke's interpretation of phrases like "baptism in the Holy Spirit" and "filled with the Holy Spirit" are given Pauline meanings and are treated as salvific and sanctifying, without any possibility of another interpretation.

    It is important to note that Paul uses the terminology "baptized in the Spirit" three times,

---

[10] Roger Stronstad, *The Charismatic Theology of St. Luke*, Hendrickson Publishers, Inc., Peabody Massachusetts, 1984, 8.
[11] Roger Stronstad, *The Charismatic Theology of St. Luke*, Hendrickson Publishers, Inc., Peabody Massachusetts, 1984, 8.

while Paul only uses it once. Yet, Paul's theology defines the terminology. Likewise, the terminology "filled with the Spirit" occurs nine times in Luke's writings and only one time in Paul's writings, yet, again, Paul's theology defines the terminology.

The point is that Paul's theology has virtually silenced Luke's teachings on the Holy Spirit. By now you may be wondering, "So what is the answer to this problem?" *The answer is to recognize that Luke is not only a historian, but a theologian in his own right.* Even though Luke is believed to have been a companion of Paul, this does not mean that he had no thoughts or theology of his own. It is totally plausible that Luke wrote with a different perspective, and with a different purpose in mind. So, we must learn to let Luke speak for himself!

When we take all of this into consideration, we can assert—with biblical and scholarly confidence—that Luke did **not** write his narrative history to highlight the salvific or sanctifying ministry of the Holy Spirit, which is in keeping with Paul, but he wrote to highlight a third dimension of Christian life—service.[12] Hence Luke's perspective of the Holy Spirit is Charismatic and **not**

---

[12] Roger Stronstad, *The Charismatic Theology of St. Luke*, Hendrickson Publishers, Inc., Peabody Massachusetts, 1984, 12.

soteriological. When we say Charismatic, we mean the perspective that "God's gift of His Spirit to His servants, either individually or collectively, is to anoint, empower, or inspire them for divine service. As recorded in the Scripture . . . this charismatic activity is necessarily an experiential phenomenon."[13]

So, we can come out of the closet and into the spotlight of what God is doing in these endtimes. We are a part of the recapturing of the Charismatic theology of Saint Luke. We stand on solid and biblical ground and in the bright light of God's revelation and love, when we pursue the baptism in the Holy Spirit for power for witnessing and transacting kingdom business, after salvation, which—in Luke–Acts—is always accompanied by inspired speech, and that speech tends to be tongues and/or prophecy!

Before we can get to the heart of this book, there is one more thing that we must touch on. Fundamentals and Evangelicals have tended to get stuck in the dispensation of The Gospels and the cross of Jesus Christ. Wait just a minute, before you accuse me of heresy. Our salvation is based upon and flows out of the cross of Christ and the Gospels give us the historical narratives that support the importance of the cross. But, the Bible doesn't end with the Gospel of John. It continues on in the history of the book of Acts. Even though we

---

[13] Roger Stronstad, *The Charismatic Theology of St. Luke*, Hendrickson Publishers, Inc., Peabody Massachusetts, 1984, 13.

are still reaping the benefits of the cross, this is the dispensation of the Holy Spirit. Conservative, American theology is doctrinally trinitarian, but practically dualistic. We say that we believe in the Father, the Son, and the Holy Spirit, but in actuality we believe in the Father, the Son, and the Holy Bible. The doctrine of the third person of the Triune Godhead is underdeveloped, if not wholly undeveloped.

This has probably come about as a reaction to the extremes of Pentecostalism. Nevertheless, that is no defense for not going "back to the Bible" and seeing what God has to say. Luke seems pretty clear that we are in the dispensation of the Holy Spirit and that these times would be characterized by the Holy Spirit. The words of Peter, in his stirring sermon on the Day of Pentecost, must be taken into more serious consideration. He said:

> But this is what was spoken of through the prophet Joel: "AND IT SHALL BE IN THE LAST DAYS," God says, "THAT I WILL POUR FORTH OF MY SPIRIT ON ALL MANKIND; AND YOUR SONS AND YOUR DAUGHTERS SHALL PROPHESY, AND YOUR YOUNG MEN SHALL SEE VISIONS, AND YOUR OLD MEN SHALL DREAM DREAMS; EVEN ON MY BONDSLAVES, BOTH MEN AND WOMEN, I WILL IN THOSE DAYS POUR FORTH OF MY SPIRIT and they shall prophesy."
>
> (Acts 2:16–18)

Preface

It is with this short, but challenging preface, that I want to draw us back to a study of the work of the Holy Spirit in the life of the sinner-believer. I will explain why I use the phraseology "sinner-believer," as we move forward.

Would you lay aside your biases for a while and seek to study the Word of God with me? I invite you to ask God to open your heart and mind and give you fresh illumination of his Word.

—Bishop Joey Johnson
Presiding Bishop of The Beth-el Fellowship
of Visionary Churches
Senior Pastor of The House of the Lord
Akron, Ohio

Acknowledgments

Special thanks to Dr. Dave Collings for his critical reading and suggestions.

Special thanks to pastors of the Beth-El Fellowship of Visionary Churches who are pushing me to write, as the Presiding Bishop of the Fellowship.

Special thanks to Bishops J. Delano Ellis, II., Timothy J. Clarke, and John Hilton for their participation in my consecration to the bishopric.

Special thanks to Pastor Jack W. Hayford; my friend and mentor.

Chapter 1

The Drawing or Wooing Work of the Holy Spirit

In working with Pastor R. A. Vernon, of The Word Church, in Maple Heights, Ohio, concerning what I believe the Bible teaches about the Holy Spirit, he urged me to put this material in book form for him and other pastors to learn from. After thinking about that request and my apostolic calling (*this is apostolic with a small "a" to indicate that it is **not** like Christ's original twelve, but simply having oversight over more than one church*) to present and defend fresh reformation or restoration Bible truth; after thinking about the fact that I have been doing a fair amount of fresh teaching about the Baptism in the Holy Spirit or the "Lukan" Filling of the Holy Spirit; after thinking about the fact that I have never given an in-depth treatment of the work of the Spirit in our lives, i.e. from His initial stirrings to our final sanctification; I believe that now is the time to make my first attempt at such a monumental task.

It has been said that we should **not** seek or overemphasize the Holy Spirit, because His work is to glorify Jesus Christ. **This is nonsense!** This is the dispensation of the Holy Spirit and when the ministry of the Holy Spirit is understood and appropriated, He, the Holy Spirit Himself, will glorify Jesus Christ and make Him more real and personal in our lives. We don't have to help the Holy Spirit carry out His ministry. We just need to release Him to do so, by yielding to Him.

Wayne Grudem, a moderately conservative theologian said, "At Pentecost believers experienced a transition from an Old Covenant experience of the Holy Spirit to a more powerful, New Covenant experience of the Holy Spirit."[14]

This is the dispensation of the Holy Spirit. Jesus has been crucified, buried, raised from the dead, and ascended, but He promised us another Helper of the same nature as Him. He said, "He is with you, but He shall be in you!" **The inauguration of this dispensation is tied up with the Holy Spirit and power.** Yet, we have been afraid to study, talk about, and teach about the Holy Spirit, because of a reaction to extreme Pentecostalism, Charismatic confusion, and emotionalism. *We can no longer be afraid of what is explicitly taught in the New Testament.*

---

[14] Wayne Grudem, *Systematic Theology: An Introduction to Biblical Theology*, Zondervan Publishing House, Grand Rapids, Michigan, 1994, 772.

The Drawing or Wooing Work of the Holy Spirit

Following is a chart that I developed to help Pastor Vernon understand what I believe the Bible says about the work of the Holy Spirit, in the life of the sinner-believer, in this new dispensation. I use the term sinner-believer,

The Work of the Holy Spirit In the Life of the Sinner-Believer	
Action	**What "The House of the Lord" (*Biblecostals*™) Believe**
The drawing or wooing work of the Holy Spirit (Jn. 6:44; Gen. 24)	Previous to Salvation
The convicting work of the Holy Spirit (*The Spirit convicts the sinner of sin, righteousness, and judgment*) (Jn. 16:7-11)	Previous to or at the Moment of Salvation
The birthing work of the Holy Spirit (Jn. 3:1-8)	At Salvation
The baptizing work of the Holy Spirit (1 Cor. 12:13)	At Salvation
The indwelling work of the Holy Spirit (1 Cor. 12:13)	At Salvation
The sealing work of the Holy Spirit (2 Cor. 1:22; Eph. 1:13; Eph. 4:30)	At Salvation
The controlling work of the Holy Spirit (filled) (Eph. 5:18)	Subsequent to Salvation, (*not viewed as the baptism in the Holy Spirit*)
The empowering work of the Holy Spirit (Baptized in the Holy Spirit [Acts 1:5]; Filled with the Spirit [Acts 2:4])	Subsequent to Salvation, (*not viewed as controlled by the Holy Spirit*)

because I believe that we are chosen by Jesus Christ, from the foundation of the world. So, the Holy Spirit begins to work with us as sinners, because we are going to be believers. Be that as it may, I will walk through these works of the Holy Spirit in eight chapters.

We begin with the drawing or wooing ministry of the Holy Spirit. Jesus states:

> No one can come to Me unless the Father who sent
> Me draws him; and I will raise him up on the last day.
> (John 6:44)

In this verse, Jesus gives a statement that has to do with sinners getting saved. He states that nobody can come to him, i.e. for salvation, unless the Father draws him; and I will raise him up on the last day. I can hear some of you saying, "This verse is not about the ministry of the Holy Spirit, but the drawing power of the Father, Jehovah God!" Ostensibly you are right, but when you look at this more deeply, it leads directly to the drawing ministry of the Holy Spirit. *Sinners are saved by the will of the Father, the sacrifice of the Son, and the effectual ministry of the Holy Spirit.* So, this is, in actuality, about the often invisible and seldom noticed drawing ministry of the Holy Spirit.

The drawing ministry of the Holy Spirit is His only ministry to sinners! I would **not** state as some have that God doesn't hear a sinner's prayer, except for the prayer of salvation, which is based upon the recorded words of a blind man who was healed, who was probably speaking to and for the Pharisees (John 9:31). But, I would state that the ministry of the Holy Spirit, in the lives of sinners, is the ministry of drawing them to salvation, according to the will of God and through the death, burial, and resurrection of Jesus Christ.

I want to state right now, "I thank God for drawing me to Himself and saving me!" I remember what Paul wrote to the Ephesians:

> *Remember* that you were at that time separate from Christ, excluded from the commonwealth of Israel, and strangers to the covenants of promise, having no hope and without God in the world. But now in Christ Jesus you who formerly were far off have been brought near by the blood of Christ.
>
> (Ephesians 2:12–13 emphasis mine)

Even though I was a child when I got saved, before that blessed moment, I was separate from Christ, excluded from the commonwealth of Israel, a stranger to the covenants of promise—especially the New Covenant, having no hope, without God in this world. But, now, in Christ Jesus, I, who was formerly far off, have been brought near by the blood of Jesus Christ. *This blessing is ours, if we have trusted Jesus Christ for salvation, because of the drawing work of the Holy Spirit.*

Unfortunately, we don't get much of a picture of the drawing work of the Holy Spirit in the New Testament.

Nevertheless, God has given us a wonderful picture of this work in the Old Testament. Very often, in the Bible, the doctrines are stated in the New Testament, while the stories, pictures, and illustrations of those doctrines are given to us in the Old Testament.

Well, the picture that I am referring to is seen in Genesis 24. The picture is captured in the first 61 verses. I would suggest that you get your Bible, turn to this passage, and read it, before you read any further in this book.

The Bible scholars seem to all be in agreement that this story is about God, Jesus Christ, the Holy Spirit, and the Church.

- Abraham pictures God the Father, the Father of Eternity and Ancient of Days.
- Isaac pictures Jesus Christ, the beloved Son.
- The servant represents the Holy Spirit.
- The Holy Spirit is the servant sent on a mission to win a bride out of the world for God's son. The servant represents the Holy Spirit, Who has charge of all that God the Father owns. We see that God sent the Holy Spirit to the country of this world to take a wife for His Son, Jesus Christ. And
- The woman represents the Church of Jesus Christ.

In the title of this chapter, I used the word "woo," because it is an old word that vividly describes the Hebrew word that is used. The Hebrew word is:

laqach "a primitive root; to *take* (in the widest variety of applications) :- accept, bring, buy, carry away, drawn, fetch, get, infold, marry, mingle, place, receive (-ing), reserve, seize, send for, take (away, -ing, up), use, **win**" (*Strong's Greek & Hebrew Dictionary*).

In this story, the meaning of the word is not "to take against the will of another," but to "win," because the servant asks Abraham what he should do if the woman was unwilling to accompany him. Abraham lets him know that he would be free of the mission or vow. *The word "woo" means "win," i.e. "to pursue the affection of another as in courting; or to solicit or entreat with importunity."*

In case you didn't read the story in your Bible, for whatever reason, let me cite two passages.

Then the servant took ten camels from the camels of his master, and set out with a variety of good things of his master's in his hand; and he arose and went to Mesopotamia, to the city of Nahor.

(Genesis 24:10)

When the camels had finished drinking, the man took a gold ring weighing a half-shekel and two bracelets for her wrists weighing ten shekels in gold, and said, "Whose daughter are you? Please tell me, is there room for us to lodge in your father's house?"

(Genesis 24:22–23)

Likewise, one day, the Holy Spirit left heaven with a variety of good things of the Master's in His hand, so that He might "draw," "woo," or "win" a bride for His Master's Son, Jesus Christ!

So, we are saved because of the drawing, wooing, winning ministry of the Holy Spirit! And how does the Holy Spirit draw and woo us? *The Holy Spirit draws and woos us through displaying to us the riches of His Master, Jehovah God and His Son, Jesus Christ.* The riches of God, the Father, and God, the Son, are seen in the riches of their lovingkindness. The Holy Spirit draws us through lovingkindness, i.e. covenant kindness, i.e. the steadfast, covenant, loyal love of God. *In the New Testament, we sometimes call this grace.*

This "grace" is beautifully stated and illustrated in the Old Testament, between God and Israel. The Bible states:

> The LORD appeared to him (*i.e. Israel*) from afar, *saying,* "I have loved you with an everlasting love; therefore I have drawn you with lovingkindness."
>
> (Jeremiah 31:3)

The word "lovingkindness" "is covenant terminology and it refers to loyal fulfillment of one's obligations previously undertaken" (*Word Biblical Commentary, 2 Samuel*). **This is lovingkindness, i.e. the kindness that we receive because of the covenant between Jesus and God, which is meant to draw us toward that One who is kind to us.**

> Or do you think lightly of the riches of His kindness and tolerance and patience, not knowing that the kindness of God leads you to repentance?
>
> (Romans 2:4)

Most people think that God draws people through trouble, and trouble may be involved for many reasons, but God often draws through the "riches of His kindness." The trouble comes because we run from His love, **not** understanding it, **not** knowing how to trust it, **not** believing that anyone could love us and treat us kindly, but the Bible is clear.

All right! We know that the Holy Spirit draws us through kindness or grace, but what does this grace look like? *Well, the Holy Spirit extends God's grace to us by offering us a dowry on behalf of God's Son, Jesus Christ.* What is that dowry? The dowry consists of gifts from God. *One of the gifts that God gives to us is the pledge or down payment of the Holy Spirit Himself.* The Bible reads:

> In Him, you also, after listening to the message of truth, the gospel of your salvation—having also believed, **you were sealed in Him with the Holy Spirit of promise, who is given as a pledge of our inheritance,** with a view to the redemption of God's own possession, to the praise of His glory.
>
> (Ephesians 1:13–14 emphasis mine)

The dowry or down payment, which guarantees our future marriage at the Marriage Supper of the Lamb, is the Holy Spirit. He has been given and we have received Him. Thank God for the Holy Spirit! We are now betrothed to Jesus Christ, as His bride, and the Holy Spirit is both the token and the guide to the Father's House, which is represented by the New Jerusalem.

Please keep this in mind: "The Holy Spirit is so dynamic that He fulfills many roles and represents many things, in the Bible."

Another class of gifts that God gives as a dowry for us is spiritual blessings. Paul wrote:

> Blessed be the God and Father of our Lord Jesus Christ, who has blessed us with every spiritual blessing in the heavenly places in Christ, just as He chose us in Him before the foundation of the world, that we would be holy and blameless before Him. In love He predestined us to adoption as sons through Jesus Christ to Himself, according to the kind intention of His will, to the praise of the glory of His grace, which He freely bestowed on us in the Beloved. In Him we have redemption through His blood, the forgiveness of our trespasses, according to the riches of His grace.
> (Ephesians 1:3–7)

Two of those spiritual blessings, which are in keeping with the riches of His grace, are redemption through His blood and the forgiveness of our sins. When you consider the Greek words that have to do with redemption, i.e. *agorazo, exagorazo,* and *lutroo,* we learn that we have been purchased in the slave market of sin, taken out of the slave market of sin, and released to never return again.

In addition, all of our sins pertaining to our salvation—past, present, and future—have been forgiven. *What a powerful truth!*

These are just two of the spiritual blessings that Paul is talking about. Lewis Sperry Chafer, organizer of Dallas Theological Seminary, said that when we are saved thirty-three different things happen to us. In other words, we receive thirty-three different spiritual blessings—and there are probably more.

So, the Holy Spirit, in the gift of Himself and the gift of salvation, has given us a sample of the riches that await us, after we are snatched from this world, led to the Father's House, celebrate at the Marriage Supper of the Lamb, and then embark on our eternal honeymoon with the Father's only begotten Son, Jesus Christ!

But, there is still another class of gifts that we need to mention. This class consists of the gifts of signs, wonders, and miracles. The writer of the Hebrews states:

> How will we escape if we neglect so great a salvation? After it was at the first spoken through the Lord, it was confirmed to us by those who heard, **God also testifying with them, both by signs and wonders and by various miracles and by gifts of the Holy Spirit** according to His own will.
>
> (Hebrews 2:3–4 emphasis mine)

These are signs, miracles, and wonders of the Holy Spirit that attest to the miracle of salvation!!!

Finally, the fourth class of gifts that God gives as a dowry for us is the gifts of the Holy Spirit. These were noted in the verses we just read. Those who had actually heard the Lord, Jesus Christ, confirmed the word of this great salvation. In addition, God bore them witness not only by signs, wonders, and various miracles, but also by gifts of the Holy Spirit. Peter tells us in 1 Peter 4:10, in the NIV, that spiritual gifts are the grace of God in various forms. **The Holy Spirit gave us spiritual gifts to continue to woo us and win us for Jesus Christ, our Bridegroom.** He is the down payment, He is the guide, He attests His mission with signs, miracles, and wonders, and He left spiritual gifts. These gifts are listed in Romans 12:3–8, 1 Corinthians 12:8–10, and Ephesians 4:11–13. Because, we may be less familiar with 1 Corinthians 12:8–10, we will touch on this list.

> For to one is given the word of wisdom through the Spirit, and to another the word of knowledge according to the same Spirit; to another faith by the same Spirit, and to another gifts of healing by the one Spirit, and to another the effecting of miracles, and to another prophecy, and to another the distinguishing of spirits, to another various kinds of tongues, and to another the interpretation of tongues.
>
> (1 Corinthians 12:8–10)

Let me briefly define the manifestation (*phanerosis*) of the Spirit, as they are referred to in 1 Corinthians 12:7.

1. The Word of Wisdom.
    A Spirit-inspired utterance that is characterized by wisdom.

2. The Word of Knowledge.
    "'The word of knowledge' is a gift of the Holy Spirit giving supernatural insight or information which one would not have known apart from the Spirit's revealing it. It differs from general biblical knowledge in that it's spontaneously revealed rather than learned through study or acquired by experience; however, it must always be tested against revealed biblical knowledge."[15]

3. Faith.
    "The manifestation of faith is the spontaneously granted spiritual ability to release the energy of God for any given action or need; it is to be differentiated from faith that leads to salvation or from general Christian faith developed through a daily walk with the Spirit."[16]
    I call this miracle-working faith.

---

[15] Jack W. Hayford, *People of the Spirit*, Thomas Nelson Publishers, Nashville, Tennessee, 1993, 123.

[16] Jack W. Hayford, *People of the Spirit*, Thomas Nelson Publishers, Nashville, Tennessee, 1993, 128.

4. Gifts of Healings.
    Sovereign instances of supernatural healing of the body, soul, or spirit of an individual or group.

5. The Workings of Miracles.
    The Sovereign display of *dunamis*, i.e. the supernatural, miracle-working power of God, beyond the gifts of healings.

6. Prophecy.
    "Spontaneous, Spirit-inspired, intelligible messages, orally delivered in the gathered assembly, intended for the edification or encouragement of the people."[17] This is contemporary prophecy and is **not** to be equated with or lifted up to the authority of canonical prophecy, which is the completed canon of the Word of God. Contemporary prophecy tends to be a fresh statement of some truth, principle, or message from the Word of God.

7. The Distinguishing of Spirits.
    The Spirit-given "ability to discern the true source of circumstances or motives of people."[18]

---

[17] Jack Hayford, *Gifts, Fruit & Fullness of the Holy Spirit*, Thomas Nelson Publishers, Nashville, Tennessee, 1993, 138.
[18] Jack W. Hayford, *Spirit-Filled Life Bible* (Nashville, TN: Thomas Nelson Publishers, 1991), 1737, note on 12:8–11.

8. Various Kinds of Tongues.

- Tongues in the book of Acts is the gift of speaking in known human languages that were **not** learned, through the power of the Holy Spirit, that accompanied the coming of the Holy Spirit to various people groups listed in Acts 1:8.
- Tongues in 1 Corinthians and modern tongues, for the most part, seem to be transrational,[19] precognitive, or preconceptual language, inspired by the Holy Spirit that tends to accompany the "Lukan" filling with the Holy Spirit, and is for giving prophetic messages when interpreted, but mostly for *private* prayer, praise, worship, and spiritual warfare.

  By *private*, I do **not** mean **never** verbalized without interpretation, but silent to the assembly or spoken to oneself and to God, i.e. whispered or in a low voice spoken and directed heavenward, as opposed to other people. (*This view is derived from the biblical and contextual study of Acts 2, 8, 10, 19, and 1 Corinthians chapters 12–14*).

---

[19] *Spirit-Filled Life Bible* (Nashville, TN: Thomas Nelson Publishers, 1991), 1737.

9. The Interpretation of Tongues.

    "Interpretation is a complementary gift which makes possible and meaningful the use of tongues in meaningful worship. Interpretation is not an accurate translation nor a commentary on the prayer in the Spirit, rather it is a presentation of the essential content in the mother tongue."[20]

These nine gifts are a part of God's dowry to us, God's guarantees, or tokens of His kindness and what He wants to do for us after the marriage is held at the Marriage Supper of the Lamb. One reason that the Holy Spirit has displayed them to us is to draw, woo, and win us to the Son of the Father.

- I thank God for the down payment of the Holy Spirit Himself.
- I thank God for the spiritual blessings of salvation.
- I thank God for the signs, wonders, and miracles.
- I thank God for the spiritual gifts that He has given to us.
- I thank God for sending the Holy Spirit to draw us unto Himself with lovingkindness!

---

[20] Arnold Bittlinger, *Gifts and Graces* (Grand Rapids, Mich.: Eerdmans, 1967), 51.

Chapter 2

The Convicting Work of the Holy Spirit

THE POWER OF A MOTHER'S PRAYERS

When Dr. R. A. Torrey was a young man, he had no faith in God or the Bible. His mother, however, was a devout Christian who constantly prayed for his conversion and often witnessed to him. One day he said to her, "I don't want to hear about my sins and your prayers; I'm going to leave and not bother you any more." With tear-filled eyes the woman followed him to the gate and pleaded with him to change his mind. But he would not be detained. Frantically she cried, "Son, you are going the wrong way, but when you come to the end of your rope and everything seems hopeless, call upon your mother's God with all your heart and He will surely help you!"

After Torrey left home, he went deeper into the ways of sin. One night in a hotel room he was unable to sleep. Weary from the problems pressing in on every hand, he decided to take the gun he kept in his dresser and end his life. Just as he reached for the weapon, he remembered his mother's last words. *Convicted by the Holy Spirit*, he fell on his knees and cried out, "O God of my mother, if there is such a Being, I need Your help. If You will help me now, I'll follow You!" In a moment his darkened heart was illumined, and peace filled his soul. Later R. A. Torrey became an outstanding evangelist who led thousands to Christ!

Earlier, I mentioned the term sinner-believer. I use that term to include the movement of the Holy Spirit in the life of the sinner, who has been elected to salvation before the foundation of the world, and then experiences the ministry of the Holy Spirit from the point of being drawn to salvation, and beyond.

This understanding is important as we consider the convicting work of the Holy Spirit. We get a glimpse of this ministry through the words of Jesus Christ:

> But I tell you the truth, it is to your advantage that I go away; for if I do not go away, the Helper will not come to you; but if I go, I will send Him to you. And He, when He comes, will convict the world concerning sin and righteousness and judgment; concerning sin, because they do not believe in Me; and concerning righteousness, because I go to the Father and you

no longer see Me; and concerning judgment, because the ruler of this world has been judged.

(John 16:7–11)

These are the words of our Lord and Savior, Jesus Christ. They were given during His midnight discourse, just prior to entering Gethsemane. Our Lord spoke these words to his sorrowing disciples about the Holy Spirit (*Willmington's Guide to the Bible*).

In these words, Jesus first promises his disciples the Helper, when He has to go away. Jesus had come to die. He had **not** come to stay on this earth. Therefore, He would soon be embarking on the last leg of His journey here on earth, which was to die for the sins of the world. He would have to leave His disciples, through death, and go back to the Father. He knew that their hearts would be broken, so He told them that it was to their advantage that He go away. His going away would mean the sending and the arriving of the Helper.

Helper 3875 *parakletos* "called to one's aid" (*NASB Greek & Hebrew Dictionary*).

The word is translated "Comforter," in the KJV. "This old word (Demosthenes) . . . was used for a legal assistant, pleader, advocate, one who pleads another's cause" (*A. T. Robertson's Word Pictures*). **The word is derived from the concept of one who is called to stand back-to-back with you in a war or battle and help you fight the battle.**

The ministry of the Holy Spirit is that of Helper, Comforter, Advocate or Lawyer, and/or Intecessor.

While Jesus was on earth, He was the disciples' Helper—but He had to go back to heaven. So, when Jesus left, He sent another Helper of the same kind as He was. The Greek word for "another" is *allos*, not *heteros*, i.e. another of the same kind, not a different kind. Jesus said:

> If you love Me, you will keep My commandments. I will ask the Father, and He will give you another Helper, that He may be with you forever.
>
> (John 14:15–16)

Now that's exciting, but there is more. He goes on to say in the next two verses:

> *That* is the Spirit of truth, whom the world cannot receive, because it does not see Him or know Him, *but* you know Him because He abides with you **and will be in you**. I will not leave you as orphans; I will come to you.
>
> (John 14:17–18 emphasis mine)

Jesus told His disciples that the Comforter or Helper would not only be **with** them, but He would be *in* them. Another Helper, of the same nature as Jesus, would abide *in* them. What a promise! And that promise has been fulfilled!! *The Helper, the Holy Spirit, now abides in us, and* *even though this has been a mystery, the illumination of this reality should bring us great hope.* Paul wrote:

> To whom God willed to make known what is the riches of the glory of this **mystery** among the Gentiles, which is **Christ in you, the hope of glory**.
> (Colossians 1:27 emphasis mine)

God comforts or helps us through the personal and intimate ministry of the indwelling Holy Spirit.

As Jesus was talking to the disciples about the Helper, He also went on to explain the Helper's ministry to the world, i.e. those who were unbelievers or unsaved.

The key word in this passage is the word "convict." In the Greek, it is *elegcho* which is elsewhere translated as follows:

To convince.

> Which of you **convinceth** me of sin? And if I say the truth, why do ye not believe me?
> (John 8:46 KJV emphasis mine)

To convict.

> And they which heard it, being **convicted** by their own conscience, went out one by one, beginning at the eldest, even unto the last: and Jesus was left alone, and the woman standing in the midst.
> (John 8:9 KJV emphasis mine)

To tell someone his fault.

If your brother sins, go and **show him his fault** in private; if he listens to you, you have won your brother.
(Matthew 18:15 emphasis mine)

Thus the holy Hound of Heaven, as He has been
called, will track down the sinner, and, upon "catching"
him/her, will (1) convince him/her; (2) convict him/her;
and (3) tell him/her his faults.

Harold Willmington, in *Willmington's Guide to the Bible*,
does such an excellent job with this Scripture and doctrine
that I am going to use his outline for our discussion.

The Helper, the Holy Spirit convicts people. Now,
from a biblical perspective, the word "convicts" means
to convince, persuade, or to demonstrate to someone
that s/he is wrong.

Now there are three things that the Holy Spirit convicts sinners of:

1. Sin.
    *Here the sin is not illicit sex, smoking, or swear-
    ing, but rejecting Christ's sacrifice on Calvary—
    i.e. the sin of not believing in or trusting Jesus Christ
    to save them. This is, of course, the one, ultimate
    sin which will damn a person's soul in hell forever.*
    Jesus said:

> He who believes in Him is not judged; he who
> does not believe has been judged already, be-
> cause he has not believed in the name of the
> only begotten Son of God.
>
> (John 3:18)

It is important to fully understand this fact. Often the seeking sinner is left confused and uncertain as to how many sins s/he must be expected to repent of to be saved? What about those sins s/he may have forgotten? Not only is this concept confusing to the *immoral* unsaved person, but it is equally confusing to the *moral* unsaved person. After all, s/he does not drink, gamble, smoke, or even fudge on his income tax report. Thus, s/he concludes s/he has **no** need of salvation. But, in fact, s/he too, like the drunkard, is guilty of rejecting Christ's sacrifice on the cross and, therefore, is in desperate need of repentance and salvation.

This is where the Holy Spirit comes in. The Spirit of God, through the Word of God and the people of God, in the context of a person's situations and circumstances, convicts, convinces, persuades, and points out the fault of **dis**believing in or **not** trusting Jesus Christ for salvation! Matthew Henry said, "The Spirit convinces of the **fact of sin**; of the **fault of sin**; of the **folly of sin**; of the **filth of sin**, that by it we are become hateful to God; of the **fountain of sin**, the corrupt nature; and lastly, of the **fruit of sin**, that the end thereof is death." Sin is so impacting and penetrating that without the convicting ministry of the Holy Spirit it would be impossible for sinners to get saved.

All right! The Holy Spirit also convicts people of:

2. Righteousness.
    What is righteousness? Righteousness has to do with rightness, justice, fairness, etc. The English word "just" implies adherence to a standard of rightness or lawfulness without reference to one's own inclinations (© 1995 Zane Publishing, Inc. © 1994, 1991, 1988 Simon & Schuster, Inc.). But, *human* justice and *divine* justice, i.e. the justice of God, are far different.

    "**In biblical usage, righteousness is rooted in covenants and relationships.** For biblical authors, righteousness is the fulfillment of the terms of a covenant between God and Humanity or between humans in the full range of human relationships" (*Holman Bible Dictionary*, Marion Soards). This is a much different concept of righteousness than what is usually put forth. So, please consider the fact that Jesus Christ is the only One who can fulfill the terms of the covenants between God and

Humanity, from the Adamic Covenant to the New Covenant. So, *Jesus is the ultimate standard of righteousness*. He is the standard of everything that is just, good, right and adequate to meet the exacting standards of Jehovah God. Yet, He was about to go back to the Father and the world would be left without the ultimate standard of righteousness. So, the Holy Spirit received the ministry of convincing, convicting, persuading, and/or telling the sinner of his/her faults with respect to righteousness. The Holy Spirit says to the sinner: "This is right, when it comes to salvation!"

Joseph Henry Thayer's Greek-English Lexicon define's righteousness as:

> Righteousness *1343 dikaiosune* "the state acceptable to God, which becomes a sinner's possession through that faith, by which he embraces the grace of God offered to him in the expiatory death of Jesus Christ."

The Holy Spirit convicts the world concerning righteousness. Using the means of the Word of God, the people of God, and the providence of God, the Spirit convicts the world of the following truths:

- the standard of righteousness, i.e. Jesus Christ, has gone back to the Father;

- that sinner is **not** righteous and has **no** righteousness in himself or herself; and
- the imputed righteousness of Jesus Christ is available by faith, provided through God's amazing grace, and offered on the basis of the expiatory, substitutionary death of Christ, upon the cross.

Again, Matthew Henry said, "The Holy Spirit proves that all the world is guilty before God. He convinces the world of righteousness; that Jesus of Nazareth was the Christ, the righteous. Also, of Christ's righteousness, imparted to us for justification and salvation. He will show them where it is to be had, and how they may be accepted as righteous in God's sight."

Even though I accepted the Lord at eight years old, I had **no** righteousness in and of myself. So, I thank God that the Holy Spirit convicted me of unrighteousness and provided for me the righteousness of Jesus, the Christ!!!

Let's move on to the third area of conviction. The Holy Spirit convicts the world of judgment.

3. Judgment.

What is judgment? Let me give you the definition of the word from the *Enhanced Strong's Lexicon*:

> "3b) sentence of condemnation, damnatory
> judgment, condemnation and punishment."[21]

The world is generally unconvinced of the fact that there is a judgment coming. Nevertheless, it is true! There is a final judgment coming and that judgment will be consummated in the judging of the present ruler of this world, i.e. the prince and power of the air, i.e. Satan, i.e. the devil. Even though his ultimate judgment awaits the Second Coming of the Messiah, he was already judged at Calvary. At Calvary, he had Jesus crucified, by the predetermined plan of Almighty God, and thought that he was victorious. But, I said, "But," three days later, Jesus got up out of the grave with all power in heaven and in earth, in His hands. *This rendered Satan judged, condemned to his future, eternal punishment, in the lake of fire and brimstone.*

So, the Holy Spirit convinces, convicts, persuades, and points out to all believing-sinners that:

1) All unsaved people belong to Satan.

> You are of your father the devil, and you
> want to do the desires of your father. He was

---

[21] *Enhanced Strong's Lexicon*, (Oak Harbor, WA: Logos Research Systems, Inc.) 1995.

a murderer from the beginning, and does not stand in the truth because there is no truth in him. Whenever he speaks a lie, he speaks from his own nature, for he is a liar and the father of lies.

(John 8:44)

There is **no** in-between or fence-sitting when it comes to Jesus and salvation. We are either saved or not; gathering with the Christ or scattering; a child of the King or a child of the devil!

The Holy Spirit also convicts the believing sinner that:

2) Satan's doom is already in the making.

The God of peace will soon crush Satan under your feet. The grace of our Lord Jesus be with you.

(Romans 16:20)

God is presently working out the details of His Kingdom, and when His Kingdom is fully established, Satan's kingdom will be destroyed. So, Satan's doom is already in the making.

This is heralded for us in "A Mighty Fortress Is Our God."

A Mighty Fortress Is Our God

(The Battle Hymn of the Reformation)

A mighty fortress is our God,
A bulwark never failing;
Our helper He, amid the flood
Of mortal ills prevailing.
For still our ancient foe
Doth seek to work us woe;
His craft and power are great,
And, armed with cruel hate,
On earth is not his equal.

And tho this world, with dev-ils filled,
Should threaten to undo us,
We will not fear, for God hath willed
His truth to triumph thru us.
The prince of darkness grim,
We tremble not for him—
His rage we can endure,
For lo! his doom is sure:
One little word shall fell him.

And though this world, with evil filled,
Should threaten to undo us;
We will not fear, for God hath willed
His truth to triumph through us.
Let goods and kindred go,
This mortal life also;

The body they may kill:
God's truth abideth still,
His kingdom is forever.

Finally, the Holy Spirit also convicts the believing sinner that:

3) All sinners will someday share his doom.

> Then He will also say to those on His left, "Depart from Me, accursed ones, into the eternal fire which has been prepared for the devil and his angels."
>
> (Matthew 25:41)

Eternal suffering in the fires of hell is the final judgment of all those who reject the substitutionary death of Jesus Christ, upon the cross. Disbelieving sinners cannot accept the fact that there is a hell, but believing sinners are brought to this realization by the Holy Spirit. This prepares them to accept the sacrifice of Jesus, on their behalf.

Hence, it is the convincing, convicting, persuading, fault-illuminating work of the Holy Spirit that leads believing-sinners to salvation in Jesus Christ.

An illustration of the convicting ministry of the Holy Spirit is seen in the book of Acts. After the *Lukan* filling of the Holy Spirit had been given, Peter stood up to preach. *The response to His sermon is a response to the convicting ministry of the Holy Spirit.*

Let's consider two Scriptures:

Men of Israel, listen to these words: Jesus the Nazarene, a man attested to you by God with miracles and wonders and signs which God performed through Him in your midst, just as you yourselves know— this *Man*, delivered over by the predetermined plan and foreknowledge of God, you nailed to a cross by the hands of godless men and put *Him* to death.

(Acts 2:22–23)

Now when they heard *this*, they were pierced to the heart, and said to Peter and the rest of the apostles, "Brethren, what shall we do?"

(Acts 2:37)

The men of Israel were pierced to the heart, i.e. they were convicted through the convicting ministry of the Holy Spirit, which was mediated through the preaching of God's man, Peter. This rendered them ready to receive salvation through the crucified Christ!

After the drawing work of the Holy Spirit, the Holy Spirit convinces, convicts, persuades, and points out to the sinner his/her sin, lack of righteousness, and final judgment, so that s/he may come to Jesus, the Christ, for salvation, imputed righteousness, and deliverance from judgment!

I am so glad that one day, He convicted me of sin, righteousness, and judgment, and now I am born again!

Chapter 3

The Birthing Work of the Holy Spirit

John 3:1–8

NEEDED: A NEW FLOOR

Charles Spurgeon, the prince of preachers, told of a missionary who visited a primitive hut and became nauseated by the filthy floor on which he had to sit. He suggested to his host that they scrub the dirty surface with soap and water, but the man replied, "The floor is just clay—packed down and dry. Add water and it turns to mud. The more you try to wash it, the worse the mess becomes!" Yes, the hut needed something besides an earthen floor.

So it is with the human heart: it is hard and dirty, and nothing will help it. We need new hearts. *We must be born again from above!* This work of the Holy Spirit is captured in the Gospel according to John 3:1–8. You may wish to read this, in your Bible, before proceeding in this chapter.

Nicodemus, a Pharisee and a ruler of the Jews, came to Jesus by night. The scholars are divided over the reason that Nicodemus came to Jesus by night. Some think that it was because he didn't wish to lose face with the other leaders, while some believe that he came at night because he was busy carrying out his considerable duties during the day and he wanted to have ample time to cover some weighty matters concerning the kingdom.

At any rate, Nicodemus starts the conversation with a statement rather than a question. His statement has to do with the obvious and perhaps is presented as an opportunity for Jesus to tell him more. Nicodemus seems to be speaking for others, probably the Pharisees and maybe the Jewish leaders, and states that he and his companions knew that Jesus was a teacher who had come from God, because **no** one could do the signs that He was doing unless God was with him. Yet, Nicodemus seems to be confused. He is probably confused, because Jesus had performed a number of attesting miracles, yet Nicodemus isn't ready to acknowledge Jesus as the Messiah. This is a little more obvious in the Greek, because the word "unless" is a conditional particle that presents a condition of the third class, which concerns a probability and **not** a fact. *Nicodemus said, more literally, "No one can do the miracles that you are doing without their being some probability that God is with you!"*

Christ's response is interesting indeed, because it doesn't seem to be connected to anything that Nicodemus said. Perhaps, Jesus knowing that Nicodemus' greatest need was salvation, cuts through the chase and goes directly to the subject of salvation.

Jesus says, "Truly, Truly," or *"Amen, Amen,* I say to you, unless one is born again, he cannot see the kingdom of God." *The words "Amen, Amen" are considered to be equal to the most solemn oath. So, the words of Jesus are of utmost importance.* No one, not even Nicodemus, a ruler of the Jews, could see or participate in the kingdom of God, without meeting certain conditions.

The phrase "born again" literally means to be born from above, i.e. born from heaven. *Since natural birth is the first birth, to be born from above or heaven is a second birth, i.e. to be born again.*

Before we get any deeper, "What Jesus said to Nicodemus is equally true for us: We must be born again, if we want to see or enter the kingdom of God!"

Now, Jesus likened the second birth or the heavenly birth to physical birth. **Physical childbirth is a radical event, experience, and change.** The child who was just before secure in the womb of its mother is thrust out into a whole new world. **Likewise, salvation is a radical event, experience, and change.** Just as a natural baby is suddenly thrust into a whole new world through the miraculous experience of being born, we, who put our trust in Jesus Christ, are suddenly thrust into a whole new world through the miraculous experience of being born again.

- We are born again!
- We are born from above!
- We are born from heaven!
- We are born into the new world of the Kingdom of God!

What a tremendous experience it was for those of us who opened our spiritual eyes for the first time!

Now Nicodemus is confused, He wants to know how he can go back into his mother's womb and be born again. Although the response seems pretty understandable, we will **not** get close to understanding this, unless we look at it from a Hebrew perspective. *I must constantly remind us that the Bible is not an American or Western book, but a Hebrew book . . . a middle-Eastern book!*

We must keep in mind that Nicodemus was a Pharisee, which means that he was a rabbi. The belief of the Pharisees has a great deal of impact upon understanding this situation. Dr. Arnold Fruchtenbaum, a saved or Messianic Jew, of Ariel Ministries, has written a fascinating pamphlet entitled *The Logos and the Rabbi*, which covers this story from a Jewish perspective. He states, "According to the Pharisees, 'All Israel has a share in the world to come.' Another part of the Pharisaic theology stated: 'Abraham sits at the gates of Gehenna to save any

Israelite consigned thereto.'"[22] *Gehenna was a garbage dumb south of Jerusalem.* It was always on fire, because of the nature of garbage under pressure, so it became the Jewish symbol for everlasting punishment. This is one of the words translated "hell" in our Bibles.

"So, according to Pharisaism, to be born a Jew physically was enough for entrance into the Kingdom. While Gentiles had to convert to Judaism, Jews themselves, by virtue of being born Jews, qualified for entrance into the Kingdom."[23]

We also know that Nicodemus was a member of the Sanhedrin, the highest Jewish court in the land. We gather this from the phrase, "a ruler of the Jews."

Now, Nicodemus, a rabbi and a member of the Sanhedrin, wanted to know how he could be born again, when he was old. Yet, he does not seem to be confused about being born again, but rather about being born again after being old. "To fully understand why he posed the question as he did, it is necessary to understand that in Pharisaic Judaism, there were six different ways of being born again. Nicodemus qualified for four of the six ways.

Let's cover first the two ways in which he was **not** qualified to be born again.

---

[22] Arnold G. Fruchtenbaum, *The Logos and the Rabbi*, Ariel Ministries, Tustin, California, 2002, 9.

[23] Arnold G. Fruchtenbaum, *The Logos and the Rabbi*, Ariel Ministries, Tustin, California, 2002, 9.

The two ways for which he was **not** qualified were:

First, when Gentiles converted to Judaism, they were said to be born again. Since Nicodemus was **not** a Gentile, he could **not** qualify in this manner.

A second way he did **not** qualify was to be crowned king, for when a man was crowned king, he was said to be born again. Nothing is said about Nicodemus having been of the House of David, and hence, he was **not** of royal lineage."[24]

"But there were four other ways to be born again, and Nicodemus qualified for all four.

First, when a Jewish boy becomes bar mitzvahed (*i.e. a ceremony that marks the beginning of manhood*) at the age of thirteen, he is said to be born again. (*I can relate to each of these events being a dynamic event and a kind of new beginning. Entering manhood is like being born again.*)

A second way was by marriage, for when a Jew was married, he was said to be born again."[25] So, when Billy Preston wrote, "Girl, with you I've been born again!" he was touting a Jewish concept. (*By the way, Billy Preston is a church musician, who crossed over to secular music.*)

"Thirdly, another way that a Jew could be born again was to be ordained as a rabbi. Since Nicodemus was a Pharisee, he had been ordained as a rabbi, and was born again in a new way.

---

[24] Arnold G. Fruchtenbaum, *The Logos and the Rabbi*, Ariel Ministries, Tustin, California, 2002, 10.

[25] Arnold G. Fruchtenbaum, *The Logos and the Rabbi*, Ariel Ministries, Tustin, California, 2002, 10.

The final way to be born again, in Judaism, was to become the head of the rabbinical school. In verse 10, Jesus said to Nicodemus that he was *the teacher of Israel*. The one who was the head of a rabbinical school was always referred to as *the teacher of Israel*. Hence, Nicodemus was also the head of a rabbinical school."[26]

"The point, then, is this: Nicodemus had undergone every process available in Judaism to be born again. *There was no other way available, in Judaism, and so the only way he could see being born again, at his age, was to re-enter his mother's womb and start the process all over again.*

It was to this problem of Pharisaic theology that Jesus addressed Himself. He clearly told Nicodemus: *Unless one is born of the water and the Spirit, he cannot enter the kingdom of God. To be born of the water was a Jewish expression for physical birth.* According to Pharisaic theology, being born of water, or being born physically as a Jew, was sufficient for entrance into the Kingdom. But Jesus told him that being born of the water was **not** enough, for one must be born of the water and the Spirit to enter into the Kingdom of God. In other words, one must be born both *physically* and *spiritually*, for physical birth by itself is **not** sufficient to provide entrance into the Kingdom."[27] This was another oath level statement.

---

[26] Arnold G. Fruchtenbaum, *The Logos and the Rabbi*, Ariel Ministries, Tustin, California, 2002, 10.

[27] Arnold G. Fruchtenbaum, *The Logos and the Rabbi*, Ariel Ministries, Tustin, California, 2002, 10–11.

Nicodemus' birth was natural, but the Kingdom of God was spiritual. To enter the spiritual Kingdom of God would require a spiritual birth! *Nicodemus would need to be born of the Spirit. This is the birthing work of the Holy Spirit.*

The Holy Spirit births us, believing-sinners, and we become newborn babes in Christ!!! This is prerequisite to us entering into the Kingdom of God. This ministry is automatically carried out, at the moment of salvation, for every believer who places his/her trust in Jesus Christ.

The Holy Spirit regenerates the believing-sinner. Paul wrote in his letter to Titus:

> He saved us, not on the basis of deeds which we have done in righteousness, but according to His mercy, by the washing of regeneration and **renewing by the Holy Spirit.**
>
> (Titus 3:5 emphasis mine)

The Holy Spirit literally recreates the believing-sinner and gives him/her the nature of God. The Holy Spirit thus functions as a divine "midwife" to the repenting sinner as He ushers him/her into the Kingdom of God (*Willmington's Guide to the Bible*).

- Praise God that we are born again
- Praise God that we are born from above.
- Praise God that we are born from heaven.
- Praise God that we are born of the Spirit.

- Praise God that we are pushed forth from the womb of the Holy Spirit!

    We who were dead in trespasses and sins, were warmly and securely nestled into the womb of the Holy Spirit, through the drawing and convicting work of the Holy Spirit. There were labor pains and contractions, as the Holy Spirit worked to birth us as newborn babes in Jesus and citizens of the Kingdom of God. Then, suddenly, we were thrust from the womb of the Holy Spirit into new life, the kingdom of God, and His marvelous light. We were slapped on our spiritual bottoms to awaken us to the marvelous new world.

Although some have taught that "being born of the water" is about being born of the Word of God, which is a possibility, the tipoff that Jesus is talking about natural birth is seen in the next statement. Jesus says, "That which is born of the flesh is flesh and that which is born of the Spirit is spirit." The two births yield different results. Being born of the flesh cannot make you spiritual and being born of the spirit does not come from the flesh. *Therefore, a second natural birth would not bring about the new birth that Jesus is talking about.*

Next, Jesus says, "Don't be amazed that I said to you, 'You must be born again' (*or from above, or of the Spirit*)." Then Jesus explains Himself further. He explains Himself by describing the new birth, i.e. the birth from above, from heaven, or of the Spirit. The Holy

Spirit can be likened to the wind, and in Greek the word *pneuma* can be translated either "wind" or "spirit." The wind blows wherever it wants to blow, and even though we can hear the sound of the wind, we can't see it. We don't know where it comes from, and we don't know where it is going. We can't see or totally understand the wind, but we know that it is real because we hear it, feel it, and see its effects.

It is the same with everyone who is born of the Spirit. The Holy Spirit works as He wishes. We cannot see Him, but we know He is active because we can hear His movement, sense His movement, and see His impact upon believing-sinners. We don't know where the Spirit comes from; we don't know where He is going; we don't know exactly how He operates; but we do know that He is the One who is working in the new birth or regeneration!!! We can't see or totally understand the Spirit, but we know He is real because we hear and see the effects of His work!

Now we still have a problem. Jesus keeps talking about the Kingdom of God. "When Jesus is talking about entering the kingdom of God, what is He talking about?" And, "Did this take place immediately or in the future?"

Well, "John the Baptist, Christ, and the apostles announced that the kingdom of national Israel was 'at hand.' (*But*), That offer was rejected. As a result the 'kingdom of heaven' (*or kingdom of God*), in its earthly manifested form, was postponed until Christ's Second Advent. **According to Matthew 13 the present Gospel age represents the mystery form of the kingdom.** Since the kingdom of heaven is none other than the rule of God on the earth, He must now be ruling to the extent of full realization of those things which are termed 'the mysteries' in the NT and which really constitute the new message of the New Testament (Lewis Sperry Chafer, *Systematic Theology*, 7:224)" (*New Unger's Bible Dictionary*). *The present kingdom is the rule or government of God in the hearts of those who have received Jesus as Savior and Lord! It is a mystery in that it is not clearly seen, except by those who have spiritual discernment.*

So, if that is the present Kingdom, what is Jesus talking about when He talks about the Kindgom coming? "When will God establish His kingdom? In one sense, the kingdom will **not** come until some unspecified time in the future (see, for example, Matthew 25:1–46). **There is a sense in which modern Christians may still look forward to the coming of the kingdom of God** (*i.e. at least its final manifestation*). *(This is the Messianic Kingdom.)*

On the other hand, Jesus also said that there is a sense in which the kingdom of God had come in His own time. 'The time is fulfilled, and the kingdom of God is at hand' (Mark 1:15). He said in an even more explicit way: 'But if I with the finger of God cast out devils, no doubt the kingdom of God is come upon you' (Luke 11:20). After Jesus had returned to heaven, the apostles did **not** continue to make the kingdom the central theme of their preaching. Instead, they began to speak of eternal life, salvation, forgiveness, and other themes. In doing this, they were **not** deserting Jesus' concern for the kingdom of God. They were simply expressing the same idea in their way. *To speak of salvation is to speak of the kingdom.*

We might express it as follows: God is graciously giving salvation as a free gift (extending His kingdom) to anyone who will receive it (enter the kingdom) through His Son Jesus Christ, and this salvation begins now (the kingdom is in the midst of you) and will be completed in the future (the kingdom will come like a thief in the night). As Paul put it, the kingdom of God is righteousness and peace and joy in the Holy Spirit (Romans 14:17)" (*Holman's Bible Dictionary*). *So, in the New Testament we have The Mystery Kingdom, at present, and The Messianic Kingdom coming in the future.*

I gave you all of that, so that you might understand that I believe the present manifestation of the Kingdom of God, i.e. The Mystery Kingdom, began on the Great Day of Pentecost. On the Great Day of Pentecost, i.e. Day of Pentecost in Acts 2, the Holy Spirit came to the earth in a whole new way. He came in a *new dispensation*, a *new dimension*, and with a *new dynamic*. On that day, His birthing work began. This is why Jesus told Nicodemus that He must be born again. He could **not** be born again at that moment, but Jesus was soon to die and send the *Paraclete*, the Helper, the Comforter, the Holy Ghost. *So, the birthing ministry of the Holy Spirit* *began on the Great Day of Pentecost and is now automatic and universal to everyone who places his/her trust in Jesus Christ for salvation.*

I thank God for the birthing work of the Holy Spirit.

Chapter 4

The Baptizing Work of the Holy Spirit

We come now to the baptizing work of the Holy Spirit. *This work of the Holy Spirit is captured in Paul's first letter to the Corinthians:*

> For even as the body is one and yet has many members, and all the members of the body, though they are many, are one body, so also is Christ. For by one Spirit we were all baptized into one body, whether Jews or Greeks, whether slaves or free, and we were all made to drink of one Spirit.
>
> (1 Corinthians 12:12–13)

In these verses, Paul also mentions another work of the Holy Spirit. He states that we were all made to drink of one spirit. This is the indwelling ministry of the Holy Spirit. We will save that ministry, until later. So, I am explaining the first three phrases of verse 13.

In my opinion, there is much misunderstanding surrounding the terms the baptism in/by/with the Holy Spirit, filled with the Holy Spirit, controlled by the Holy Spirit, indwelled by the Holy Spirit, etc. As I have studied these terms and their corresponding biblical references, I have determined that the authors are describing various facets of the work of the Holy Spirit. To reduce the confusion and strive for clarity, I have developed and I am going to use different terminology than is used by others. I do this in an attempt to be as clear as possible and to standardize my terminology.

So, when I use the phrase the "baptizing work of the Holy Spirit," I will be discussing what Paul is talking about in this passage before us, i.e. 1 Corinthians 12:12–13. This is the fourth work of the Spirit in the chart I gave to you earlier.

Let me begin by differentiating between 1 Corinthians 12:12–13 and Acts 1:4–5. Luke wrote:

> Gathering them together, He commanded them not to leave Jerusalem, but to wait for what the Father had promised, "Which," He said, "you heard of from Me; for John baptized with water, **but you will be baptized with the Holy Spirit** not many days from now."
>
> (Acts 1:4–5 emphasis mine)

I readily admit that Paul could be describing the same work that Luke is describing in Acts 1:5, and I accept those who hold to a doctrine in keeping with that possibility. But, after much study, I don't believe that is the case. *Let that suffice for now and be aware of the fact that I am not discussing Acts 1:4–5 in this chapter. I am only discussing 1 Corinthians 12:12–13.*

Before we can begin to plumb the depth of this teaching, we must understand the context of Paul's statements. The twelfth chapter of 1 Corinthians has to do with the *phanerosis* or manifestation of the Holy Spirit. But, the *immediate* context of verses 12 and 13 is the unity of the body. This is clearly seen in verse 12. In this verse, Paul uses the metaphor of the human body to discuss diversity in unity or many members, but one body. Paul discusses the fact that even though there is one body, yet the body has many members, and yet, even though there are many members, there is still only one body. The human body has a number of organs, hundreds of bones, billions of blood vessels, etc., yet there is only one body. He then states, "So also is Christ."

Although there are many members of the body of Christ, there is only one body of Christ!

Then Paul moves from the fact to the reason. The reason for the unity of the body is introduced by the particle "for." The Greek particle is *gar. Strong's Greek & Hebrew Dictionary* says, "a primary particle; properly assigning a *reason* (used in argument, explanation or intensification; often with other particles)." *So, the reason that we are one body, despite being many members is about to be given. The reason given is captured in the words, "For by one Spirit we were all baptized," i.e. every genuine believer in Christ—without exception, "into the one body of Christ," regardless of ethnicity or socio-economic status.* The proposition translated "by," is given a footnote in my Bible, where the possibility of "in" is added. The Greek proposition *en* can mean "by," "in," or "with," depending upon context, but all of the major translations translate this preposition as "by." In this context, the preposition has to do with instrumentality. So, by the instrumentality of the Holy Spirit, every believer is baptized into the body of Christ. *So, the reason that we are one body, despite being many members, is because of the baptizing work of the Holy Spirit.*

The word "baptized" is the transliteration of the Greek word *baptizo*, and **not** the definition of the word. To transliterate a word from one language to another is to bring it over almost letter for letter, i.e. *baptizo* to baptize. The *definition* of the word *baptizo* is to make wet, fully immerse in, or introduce into. *So, by the instrumentality of the Holy Spirit, every believer is fully immersed in the body of Christ.*

The preposition that is translated "into" is different here than in Luke's writings, when he discusses *the baptism in the Holy Spirit*, which may be another tip-off that Paul is **not** discussing the same thing that Luke is discussing.

- Luke uses the proposition *en*, and the place is the Holy Spirit.
- Paul uses preposition *eis*, and the place is the body of Christ.

The body of Christ is the place that all believers are introduced into through the baptizing work of the Holy Spirit. We are made one body through the baptizing work of the Holy Spirit.

If you didn't get that, let me come at it again from another angle.

- The agent or performer of this baptism is the Holy Spirit.
- The sphere or location of this baptism is in the body of Christ.
- The purpose is the unity of the Body.

In Acts 1:4–5, which we shall cover:

- The agent or performer of that baptism is Jesus Christ.
- The sphere or location is the Holy Spirit.
- The purpose is for power to be a witness and transact Kingdom business.

Paul also talks about this baptism by the Spirit, in other letters that he wrote. Let's touch on a few of those verses, in another letter.

Or do you not know that all of us who have been baptized into Christ Jesus have been baptized into His death? Therefore we have been buried with Him through baptism into death, so that as Christ was raised from the dead through the glory of the Father, so we too might walk in newness of life. For if we have become united with Him in the likeness of His death, certainly we shall also be in the likeness of His resurrection.

(Romans 6:3–5)

The use of the word "baptism" here is somewhat confusing and therefore debatable. Some scholars think that Paul is discussing water baptism and some think he is talking about the baptizing work of the Holy Spirit. While others think that Paul is discussing both water baptism and spiritual baptism, with water baptism being a picture of the spiritual reality.

I believe that Paul is talking about the spiritual reality of the baptizing work of the Holy Spirit. When anyone accepts Jesus Christ as his/her personal Savior, s/he is baptized into Christ Jesus or into the body of Jesus Christ. Paul asks the Romans a poignant, rhetorical question, "Do you not know that all of us who have been baptized into Christ Jesus have been baptized into His death?" *When we are baptized by the Holy Spirit, into the body of Christ, we are also baptized into His death. Because we become a part of Christ's body, His experiences become our experiences.*

78

- His death becomes our death.
- His resurrection becomes our resurrection.
- His life becomes our life.
- His victory becomes our victory (*although not fully realized until the final manifestation of the Kingdom*).
- His reign becomes our reign (*although yet future*).

Paul does **not** stop there, but goes on to talk about the implications of being baptized into the death of Jesus Christ. The implications of being baptized into the death of Jesus Christ are introduced by the word "therefore." As Paul begins to give us the implications of being baptized into Christ's death, he changes metaphors from being baptized into Christ's death to being buried with Christ, because water baptism and spirit baptism can be likened to burial. Remember, we are dealing only with the baptizing work of the Holy Spirit. *As the believing-sinner is baptized into the body of Christ, through the baptizing work of the Holy Spirit, s/he is positionally buried with Christ, into His death.*

The next words, "so that," introduce the purpose for being buried with Christ, into His death. We are buried with Christ "so that" as He was raised from the dead, through the glory of the Father, to a newness of life, we too might be raised to walk in the newness of life. *Let me underscore this, "We are buried with Christ so that we might be resurrected from the dead, to walk in the newness of life, so that God might be glorified!"*

This is so important that I am going to belabor the point. When we got saved, the Holy Spirit submerged us into the body of Christ. This baptism buried us with Christ, into His death, so that we might be resurrected from the dead, even as Jesus was resurrected from the dead, to walk in the newness of life—all for the glory of God!

Now Paul doesn't stop there, but goes on to give a very encouraging realization, "If we have been united with Him in the likeness of His death, certainly we shall also be in the likeness of His resurrection." Water baptism is a picture of dying with Jesus, being buried with Jesus, and being resurrected with Jesus. Likewise, if we are united with Christ in the likeness of His death, through the baptizing work of the Holy Spirit, we shall also be united to Him in the likeness of His resurrection, through the same baptizing work of the Holy Spirit.

Therefore, the baptizing work of the Holy Spirit introduces us into a vital new connection with Jesus, the Christ and the benefits of the ministry of Jesus, the Christ.

Another Bible verse that touches on the baptizing work of the Holy Spirit reads:

> For all of you who were baptized into Christ have clothed yourselves with Christ.
>
> (Galatians 3:27)

This Scripture is probably about water baptism. *Remember that water baptism is an outward picture of an inward reality.* So, when people accept Jesus Christ as their personal Savior and are baptized in water, the spiritual reality is stated in the metaphor of clothing themselves with Christ. *Being clothed with Christ is putting on Christ, putting on the character, interests, and manners of Christ, which is one outcome of being baptized or immersed into the body of Christ.*

Armed with this teaching, let's return to our text in 1 Corinthians 12:12–13c. Every believer in Jesus Christ has been baptized into the body of Christ, through the baptizing work of the Holy Spirit, but we are left with two very interesting questions: 1) When did this take place? and 2) when does it take place now?

Let's answer the first question. This baptizing work of the Holy Spirit probably began on the Great Day of Pentecost. Notice that the verb "baptized" is in *aorist* tense. The *aorist* tense "presents an occurrence in summary, viewed as a whole from the outside, without regard for the internal make-up of the occurrence. It may be helpful to think of the *aorist* as taking a snapshot of the action while the imperfect (like the present) takes a motion picture, portraying the action as it unfolds?"[28] So, Paul is saying that every believer was baptized into one body, i.e. the body of Christ, through the baptizing ministry of the Holy Spirit, and the whole action seems to be in the past. When in the past? The most likely

---

[28] Wallace, D. B. 1999, c1996. *Greek Grammar Beyond the Basics : An Exegetical Syntax of the Greek New Testament* (electronic ed.). Galaxie Software: Garland, TX.

choice is The Great Day of Pentecost. Pentecost is viewed as the Birthday of the Church, because there could be **no** Church until Jesus had gone away and the Helper or Comforter had come. The Great Day of Pentecost is commonly called the Birthday of the Church, because the New Testament Church is that group of people, from Pentecost to the historically, biblical rapture, who are organically joined together by the baptizing work of the Holy Spirit.

The baptizing work of the Holy Spirit is what makes us the Church and separates us from all other groups of believers!

This answers the question, "When did the baptizing work of the Holy Spirit begin?" Now we need to answer the question, "When does this baptism take place today?"

The baptizing work of the Holy Spirit that took place on the New Testament Great Day of Pentecost seems to be normative. Therefore, everyone who accepts Jesus Christ as his/her personal Savior, from the Great Day of Pentecost forward, is automatically baptized into the body of Christ, through the baptizing work of the Holy Spirit. *The transaction is automatic and universal in the Church Age.*

I thank God for the baptizing work of the Holy Spirit!

Now this causes a fair amount of confusion concerning the different ministries of the Holy Spirit, because of the dynamic nature of The Great Day of Pentecost. The Great Day of Pentecost is a watershed moment in the history of the church. On The Great Day of Pentecost, when the Holy Spirit came to the earth in an entirely new way, there also appeared a whole new spiritual dispensation, dimension, and dynamic!!!

- A "dispensation" is a divine epoch or time in which a religious doctrine or practice is believed to be in force.
  There are both new doctrines and new practices beginning on The Great Day of Pentecost.
- A "dimension" is a new level of reality, consciousness, or existence.
  There is a new level of reality, in the Spirit; a new level of consciousness, because of the Holy Spirit; and a new level of existence, in the Holy Spirit.
- A "dynamic" is a new energy, enthusiasm, or sense of purpose and ability to get things going and get things done.
  There is a new energy, enthusiasm, and power, through the Holy Spirit, from the Great Day of Pentecost forward. Wayne Grudem said, "At Pentecost believers experienced a transition from an Old Covenant experience of the Holy Spirit to a more powerful, New Covenant experience of the Holy Spirit."[29]

---

[29] Wayne Grudem, *Systematic Theology: An Introduction to Biblical Theology*, Zondervan Publishing House, Grand Rapids, Michigan, 1994, 772.

On the Great Day of Pentecost, similar to the event of salvation, many things took place. As I stated earlier, Lewis Sperry Chafer, founder of Dallas Theological Seminary, said that thirty-three different things happen when we accept Jesus as our personal Savior: justification, regeneration, initial sanctification, forgiveness of sins, etc., etc., etc. *Well, on the Great Day of Pentecost, because of its importance in the plan of God, a number of things also took place.* I believe at least five major things happened on the Great Day of Pentecost:

1. Believers were born of the Spirit of God.
2. Believers were baptized into the body of Christ, by the Holy Spirit.
3. Believers were indwelled by the Holy Spirit.
4. Believers were sealed until the day of redemption.
5. Believers were baptized in the Holy Spirit or filled with the Holy Spirit, from a "Lukan" perspective, by Jesus Christ.

So, one of the things that we must realize about the Great Day of Pentecost is that it is a day like no other in the history of the Church. And one of the things that begins on the Great Day of Pentecost is the baptizing work of the Holy Spirit, whereby we are baptized into the body of Christ!

I want to remind you that it has been said that we should **not** seek or overemphasize the Holy Spirit, because His work is to glorify Jesus Christ. This is nonsense. This is the dispensation of the Holy Spirit and when the ministry of the Holy Spirit is understood and appropriated, He, the Holy Spirit Himself, will glorify Jesus Christ and make Him more real and personal in our lives. We don't have to help the Holy Spirit carry out His ministry. We just need to release Him to do so, by yielding to Him.

Chapter 5

The Indwelling Work of the Holy Spirit

We come now to the indwelling work of the Holy Spirit. This work of the Holy Spirit is also captured in Paul's first letter to the Corinthians:

> For even as the body is one and yet has many members, and all the members of the body, though they are many, are one body, so also is Christ. For by one Spirit we were all baptized into one body, whether Jews or Greeks, whether slaves or free, and we were all made to drink of one Spirit.
>
> (1 Corinthians 12:12–13)

We have already covered the first three phrases of verse 13, which have to do with the baptizing work of the Holy Spirit. We are now going to work on the last phrase of verse 13, as it relates to the indwelling work of the Holy Spirit.

Paul states here that we were all made to drink of one Spirit, i.e. obviously the Holy Spirit. The tense and voice of this verb is the same as the word "baptized." We studied this in the last chapter. We are **not** going to worry about the voice, but we are just going to touch on the tense. The tense here is again the *aorist* tense. So the action here is viewed as summary action or as if the action took place in a snapshot, and this snapshot was taken sometime in the past. *So, every person that accepts Jesus Christ is given to drink of one Spirit, i.e. the Holy Spirit.*

Now, when we drink something, we take it inside of ourselves. I believe the phrase "we were made to drink of one Spirit," refers to the indwelling of the Holy Spirit. So, we are talking about the indwelling work or ministry of the Holy Spirit.

Keep in mind that Paul is explaining the basis for his teaching that although there are many members of the body, there is only one body of Christ, i.e. one Church. The basis of our unity is the fact that Jesus, through the instrumentality or means of the Holy Spirit, baptized us into one body and we were all made to drink of one Spirit. *I believe Paul is saying, "Because we were all baptized into one body by the Holy Spirit and we have all drunk of or are indwelled by the same Holy Spirit, we are one body!" Whether we are Baptist, Methodist, Episcopalian, Pentecostal, etc., there is but one body of Christ. So, we should*

*stop fighting against each other. The indwelling of the same
Holy Spirit makes us one!*

Now, let's begin to try to take in some of the blessings of this work of the Holy Spirit. We won't be able to
cover the many blessings of this work, because of the
scope of this work, but let's cover some.

First, according to the text before us, the Holy
Spirit not only joins us to the Savior, by baptizing us
into the body of Christ, but He also joins Himself to
us, by indwelling us. Jesus touches on this in John's
account of the Gospel:

> Now on the last day, the great day of the feast, Jesus
> stood and cried out, saying, "If anyone is thirsty, let
> him come to Me and drink. He who believes in Me,
> as the Scripture said, 'From his innermost being will
> flow rivers of living water.'" But this He spoke of the
> Spirit, whom those who believed in Him were to re-
> ceive; for the Spirit was not yet given, because Jesus
> was not yet glorified.
>
> (John 7:37–39)

On the last day of the Feast of Tabernacles, which was
the great day of the feast because it was a Sabbath day and
the last feast day of the year, "the priest, as was done on
every day of this festival, brought forth, in golden vessels,
water from the stream of Siloah, which flowed under the
temple-mountain, and solemnly poured it upon the altar" (Olshausen). As the priest poured this water upon

the altar, Jesus stood up and cried out saying, "If anyone is thirsty, let Him come to me and drink." *Jesus said, in effect, "I, in contradistinction to what you are seeing, am the water of life!"*

I am not going to elaborate on this, but if anyone is going to come to Jesus for a drink, s/he must be conscious of his/her thirst. This is captured in our church's Vision Statement by the phrase "consciously hurting." *Only those who are consciously hurting come to Jesus! People who are unconscious or unaware of their thirst/pain, don't know that they need to come to Jesus.*

Be that as it may, Jesus goes on to say, "He who believes in Me, as the Scripture said, 'From His innermost being will flow rivers of living waters.'" It is difficult to tell from the Greek whether this refers to Christ's innermost being or the believer's innermost being. *In either case, the living water will eventually make its way into and out of the innermost being of the believer.* This reality is affirmed by John's commentary. John commented that Jesus was talking about the Holy Spirit, whom those who believed in Him were to receive, for the Holy Spirit was not yet given, because Jesus was **not** yet glorified.

Therefore, after Jesus was glorified, the Holy Spirit would be given to all those who believe in Jesus Christ. This could refer to both the indwelling of the Holy Spirit and the "Lukan" filling of the Holy Spirit. *All that we are going to talk about today is the indwelling of the Holy Spirit.*

By the way, the fact that the Holy Spirit was not given until after Jesus was glorified, takes care of the Scripture that says that Jesus breathed on His disciples and said receive the Holy Spirit. Jesus was not glorified until His final ascension, so the Holy Spirit was not "officially" given, until the Great Day of Pentecost. Therefore, when Jesus said to the disciples, "Receive the Holy Spirit," He had to be referring to either a temporary indwelling or a future indwelling. I lean towards the view that when Jesus breathed upon His disciples they received a *temporary* indwelling of the Holy Spirit, until the *regularized* indwelling of the Holy Spirit would begin at Pentecost. *Jesus had been their Keeper. Now, the temporary indwelling would keep them until Pentecost!*

Please understand that the Holy Spirit, in our human spirits, produces a flow of life that touches others. Now this perpetual flow of life must flow from an internal, indwelling source. Jesus touched on this earlier, in the Gospel according to John:

> But whoever drinks of the water that I will give him shall never thirst; but the water that I will give him will become in him a well of water springing up to eternal life.
>
> (John 4:14)

The Holy Spirit is a permanently, indwelling well or source of life-giving water that will overflow the human spirit, the soul, and the body and touch the lives of others!

Let me say it again, "The indwelling of the Holy Spirit is a source of life that sustains us and touches others."

Let's move to another important verse of Scripture.

> I will ask the Father, and He will give you another Helper, that He may be with you forever; that is the Spirit of truth, whom the world cannot receive, because it does not see Him or know Him, but you know Him because He abides with you and will be in you.
>
> (John 14:16–17)

Jesus tells his disciples that He will ask the Father to give them another Helper, just like Himself, to be with them forever. This Helper is the Spirit of Truth. The world cannot receive the Spirit of Truth, because it does **not** see Him or know Him, but He reminds the disciples that they knew Him, because He was abiding with them and would be in them. *The Devil is the father of lies who propagates the spirit of error versus Jesus sending the Spirit of Truth.*

This was before the dispensation of the Church and the Holy Spirit, therefore the Holy Spirit did **not** permanently indwell anyone, at this time. Nevertheless, Jesus states that the Holy Spirit was abiding *with* the disciples, and prophesies that the Spirit of Truth would be *in* them. When would the Holy Spirit be in them? The Holy Spirit would be in them or indwell them, permanently, after His crucifixion, resurrection, ascension, and glorification! *Therefore, since this is after these events, the Spirit* *of Truth now permanently indwells us.* Consequently, we can depend upon the Holy Spirit to reveal the truth to us. He will lead us and guide us into all truth. He will never leave us without a revelation of (*substitute illumination for revelation if you hold to a more conservative view of the revelation, reception, illumination and preservation of the Word of God*) and a witness to biblical truth.

We are limited in our perception and conception of many biblical truths, because of sin, or the fact that our views and values are based on denominational or sectarian dogma, or culture, or some other limiting factor.

Another important Scripture is:

> After a little while the world will no longer see Me, but you will see Me; because I live, you will live also. In that day you will know that I am in My Father, and you in Me, and I in you.
>
> (John 14:19–20)

In these verses, Jesus, prior to His crucifixion, predicts both the baptizing work of the Holy Spirit and the indwelling work of the Holy Spirit.

He states that after a little while the world will no longer see Him, because He was going back to His father, after the crucifixion, burial, resurrection, and ascension. Nevertheless, His disciples would see Him, because of their spiritual vision and discernment. In addition, Jesus assures His disciples that because He lives, i.e. He would be living after the resurrection, they would also live through Him. *We do not understand or experience that life, because we have truncated the life and ministry of Jesus to the event of the cross. But, did you notice that because He lives—we live. I thank God for Christ's death, but I also want Jesus to live in me and through me now!*

Jesus doesn't stop there, but prophesies that in that day, i.e. on the Great Day of Pentecost, His disciples would know or come to perceive that He was in the Father, that His disciples were in Him—i.e. through the baptizing work of the Holy Spirit—, and that He was in them, through the indwelling work of the Holy Spirit.

The indwelling Holy Spirit makes the presence of Jesus Christ more real and experiential, because the Holy Spirit is—among other things—the Spirit of Christ (Rom. 8:9)!

Now, let's move on to other Scriptures. In Paul's first letter to the Corinthians, he states:

> Now we have received, not the spirit of the world, but the Spirit who is from God, so that we may know the things freely given to us by God.
>
> (1 Corinthians 2:12)

This is the spirit of the world versus the Spirit of God! Just as the Corinthian believers, we have received the Holy Spirit who is from God. The Holy Spirit indwells us and reveals or illuminates to us things that are freely given to us by God! *Thank God for the revelatory minis-*

try of the indwelling Holy Spirit. When we read the Bible, He reveals or illuminates the heart of God to us.

I hope you are beginning to appreciate the indwelling Holy Spirit. The next important Scripture states:

> Or do you not know that your body is a temple of the Holy Spirit who is in you, whom you have from God, and that you are not your own?
>
> (1 Corinthians 6:19)

Paul, in a rhetorical question to the Corinthians, reminds them that each of their bodies was a temple, i.e. the *naos*, the sacred edifice or structure, which included the Holy Place and the Most Holy Place or Holy of Holies of the Holy Spirit, who was in each of them, whom they received from God. Therefore, they were not their own, but belonged to God. Paul is likening the Holy Spirit dwelling in us to the dwelling of the Holy Spirit in the Holy of holies of a temple. Do you remember how the Shechinah or visible glory of God dwelled in the Holy of holies of The Temple of Solomon or the Mosaic Tabernacle as a pillar of cloud by day and a pillar of fire by night? Well, our human spirits are the Holy of holies of our souls, which indwell our bodies and the Holy Spirit indwells our human spirits in the same way as He indwells the Holy of holies of Old Testament houses of God. *Each of us is the permanent dwelling place of the personal presence and Shechinah glory of Jehovah God, in the person of the Holy Spirit. The Glory of God resides permanently inside us. We have this treasure in earthen vessels (2 Corinthians 4:7)!*

Now in order for the glory to shine out, our vessels must be broken—as Gideon and his soldiers metaphorically broke the pitchers that held or shielded the light of the lamps or torches that they were holding (Judges 7:20).

The next highly important Scripture reads:

> However, you are not in the flesh but in the Spirit, if indeed the Spirit of God dwells in you. But if anyone does not have the Spirit of Christ, he does not belong to Him.
>
> (Romans 8:9)

Keep in mind that Paul's subject here is walking in the flesh versus walking in the Spirit. He had just stated that those who were in the flesh could **not** please God, when he begins to touch on the contrasting position with the particle "however." He goes on to state that the Romans were not in the flesh, but in the Spirit, if or in view of the fact that the Holy Spirit dwelled in them. The word "if" is a conjunction that means "in view of the fact" or "since."

This indwelling is so important that Paul adds that anyone who does not have the Spirit of Christ does **not** belong to Christ. *So, everyone who belongs to Christ or is saved is indwelled by the Holy Spirit, who makes it possible for them to walk in the Spirit.*

Let me touch on one more major Scripture. John wrote:

The one who keeps His commandments abides in
Him, and He in him. We know by this that He abides
in us, by the Spirit whom He has given us.

(1 John 3:24)

John teaches that every one of us who keeps God's
commandments abides in God and God abides in us,
individually. Furthermore, John states that we know
that we abide in God and God abides in us because of
the Holy Spirit whom God has given to us. *It is through
the indwelling Holy Spirit that we come to perceive the
reality that we are in God, and that God permanently
abides in us.*

- Check the Spirit inside of you and verify the fact
  that God is in you.

*This is knowledge that is above the mind, above the
feelings, and above the conscience. This is knowledge that
comes from the Spirit through our human spirits. It is not
irrational; it is transrational!*

If you read a little further, John puts it like this

These things I have written to you who believe in the
name of the Son of God, so that you may know that
you have eternal life.

(1 John 5:13)

This is a "know so" salvation! Some things we think in our thinkers! Some things we feel in our feelers! But, some things we can only know in our knowers!!! This is intuitive knowledge! *Intuition is a faculty of the human spirit, that is informed by the eternal, Holy Spirit!!!*

Now, we still have the same two questions that we asked and answered with respect to the baptizing work of the Holy Spirit: 1) When did this take place? and 2) when does it take place now?

According to John 7:37–39, the Holy Spirit would be given after Jesus was glorified. When specifically? On the Great Day of Pentecost.

Therefore, on the Great Day of Pentecost, the Holy Spirit indwelled every believer and that action became normative. Once again, because this is the inauguration of a whole new dispensation, believers are permanently indwelled by the Holy Spirit. In the old dispensation, the Holy Spirit came upon or within God's people for the purpose of ministry and then left. This is seen most clearly in the life of Samson. When the Holy Spirit would come upon him, he would perform great feats of strength. Then the Holy Spirit would depart from him. *Now, every believer is permanently indwelled by the Holy Spirit as a function of and support of the gift of salvation.*

I thank God that He has given me His permanent presence, through the ministry of the indwelling Holy Spirit!

Chapter 6

The Sealing Work of the Holy Spirit

In the Roman world and kingdom, Caesar had a
seal. When the seal was affixed to anything, it
denoted the authority and ownership of Caesar. This seal
was often used to close things until one with the proper
authority could come, break the seal, and open that which
was closed. Greek scholar, A. T. Robertson, seems convinced that when Jesus was crucified, His tomb was sealed
with the seal of Caesar, meaning that no one should open
that tomb except an authorized representative of Caesar.
Whether that seal was Caesar's seal or the seal of someone else, early one Sunday morning, God broke the seal
and rolled the stone away! This was not so much so Jesus
could get out, but that the world would be able to look in
and see the miracle of the resurrection.

99

Similarly, the Bible teaches us that we are sealed, by the Holy Spirit, with heaven's seal, which denotes that we belong to God and His authority protects us from any tampering, until the authorized representative, Jesus Christ, shall come to redeem us.

Now, we come to the sealing work of the Holy Spirit. This work of the Holy Spirit is captured in a number of outstanding Scriptures. Let's work our way through some of the more important ones, in biblical order. Paul wrote:

> Now He who establishes us with you in Christ and anointed us is God, who also sealed us and gave us the Spirit in our hearts as a pledge.
> (2 Corinthians 1:21–22)

It's a shame that more sermons are **not** preached from Paul's second letter to the Corinthians. This is probably because it is more autobiographical than Paul's first letter to the Corinthians. Nevertheless, it contains some powerful truth. In these verses, Paul makes a powerful statement. "Now, He who is establishing us (*present tense*), i.e. Paul and his companions, with you, in Christ, and has anointed us (*aorist tense*), is God."

- It was God who was establishing Paul and His companions with the Corinthians believers, in Christ.

- It was God who was confirming Paul and his companions in a sure state of salvation, along with the Corinthians in Christ.

The Greek word translated "with" denotes a close association or relationship. So, it could be translated, "Now He who establishes us *together with* you, in Christ . . ." The phrase "in Christ" is distinctively Pauline, i.e. characteristic of Paul, and relates to the sphere of salvation or genuine belief in Christ. The verb "establishes" is in the active tense, but the second verb "anoint" is in the *aorist* tense. The word "anoint" means to literally apply oil. *When used of the Holy Spirit, it means to consecrate with the receiving of the Holy Spirit.*

Although God was in the process of establishing Paul and His companions with the Corinthians, He had already anointed them with the Holy Spirit sometime in the past, with the results of that anointing continuing into the present.

So, we assume that this anointing took place on the Great Day of Pentecost.

Paul does **not** stop there but continues his statement. Not only was God establishing them in Christ and had anointed them with the Holy Spirit, He had also sealed them and given them the Holy Spirit in their hearts as a pledge. Both the verbs "sealed" and "gave" are also in the *aorist* tense. Even as the anointing took place in the past, probably on the Great Day of Pentecost, so this sealing and giving of the Holy Spirit must have also taken place sometime in the past—probably on the Great Day of Pentecost.

Now, a seal was placed on things to prevent them from being opened. Only the person or group who placed a seal on something was authorized to open that seal. Christ's borrowed tomb was not to be opened, except by the person or group that placed that seal upon it.

Another way of looking at a seal is as signature. By way of example, the Roman seal was likely a wax that was imprinted with the seal or ring of Caesar. That imprint was like a signature and only the one who had that signature had a right to open the borrowed tomb of Christ.

Likewise, Christ sealed the Corinthian believers with the seal of the Holy Spirit. He placed His seal or wrote His signature over the hearts of the Corinthians, through the Holy Spirit, and sealed them from tampering. This certainly applies to every believer, hence it applies to us. *We have been sealed and signed by the Holy Spirit. This prevents anyone from opening us up or tampering with us, until the Sealer and Signer returns!*

In addition, to verify that the seal or signature was legitimate, God also gave the Corinthians the Holy Spirit as a pledge or down payment, until Jesus would return to open them for Himself. The KJV says that God has given us the "earnest" of the Holy Spirit. The word "earnest" is the abbreviation of an Old English phrase "earnest money," which today we call a pledge or a down payment. The pledge or down payment or token of God's return is the indwelling Holy Spirit.

There is a lot of truth in these verses, but I am only dealing with the sealing ministry of the Holy Spirit. Think about it! When we got saved, God sealed us with the Holy Spirit of promise. He wrote His name upon us, *Jehovah God*, in the ink of the Holy Spirit, which prevents anyone from tampering with the seal or opening us up, until Jesus comes. That signature is probably on our souls, but there is coming a day, and it may even be true now, that the signature will be on our foreheads. John wrote:

> There will no longer be any curse; and the throne of God and of the Lamb will be in it, and His bond-servants will serve Him; they will see His face, and **His name will be on their foreheads.**
>
> (Revelations 22:3–4 emphasis mine)

Can you imagine that signature on your forehead? *It says, like those sweatshirts we see, "Property of Jesus Christ!" and the signature, Jehovah God.* You may not be able to see it, because it takes the special lighting, illumination, or discernment of the Holy Spirit.

When you go to Disney World and you decide to leave, if you want to return later, they stamp your hand with a stamp so that you won't have to pay a second time—i.e. if you decide to return on the same day. But, the imprint cannot be seen with the naked eye. It takes an infrared light to be able to see the special ink that is used.

Likewise, we have been stamped upon our foreheads with the special ink of the Holy Spirit, but when the time is right that stamp will be revealed with the special light of the Holy Spirit. We are sealed until Jesus comes back to redeem us!

At the same time, God has given us the gift of the indwelling Holy Spirit as a pledge, token, down payment, or guarantee that He is coming back to redeem us. Every time we sense the Holy Spirit on the inside, it should be a reminder of the words of Jesus Christ:

> If I go and prepare a place for you, I will come again and receive you to Myself, that where I am, there you may be also.
>
> (John 14:3)

Every time the Holy Spirit stirs inside of us, we should hear Jesus saying, "I am coming back to get you!"

Let's move on to the next important Scripture.

> In Him, you also, after listening to the message of truth, the gospel of your salvation—having also believed, you were sealed in Him with the Holy Spirit of promise, who is given as a pledge of our inheritance, with a view to the redemption of God's own possession, to the praise of His glory.
>
> (Ephesians 1:13–14)

The words "in Him" are more literally "in whom" and refer to Jesus Christ, who was the subject of the last paragraph.

Paul says to the Ephesians, "You also, after listening to the message of truth, the Gospel of your salvation—having also believed, you were sealed in Him with the Holy Spirit of promise." *Now we are able to more accurately connect the sealing ministry of the Holy Spirit with the event of salvation, which began on the Great Day of Pentecost.* The Ephesians, after listening to the message of truth, which was the Gospel of their salvation, having also believed, they were sealed in Christ with the Holy Spirit of promise. Notice that the Ephesians could not just listen to the message of truth, they had to also believe the message of truth. Please note that the verbs "after listening," "having also believed," and "were sealed" are all in the *aorist* tense. These things all took place in the past, apparently at the same time, with results that were persisting into the present. *So, sometime in the past, the Ephesians heard the Gospel, believed it, and were sealed with the Holy Spirit of promise, i.e. the Holy Spirit that was promised by God and Jesus Christ.*

We have already talked about the fact that this probably began on the Great Day of Pentecost, but the fact that these actions all seem to happen at the same time, or at least in conjunction with one another, seems to indicate a normative experience. Other scholars also believe this to be the case.

Therefore, since the sealing of the Holy Spirit is a normative transaction that began on the Great Day of Pentecost, now every believer who listens to the message of truth, the Gospel of salvation, and believes that message, is sealed, in Christ, with the Holy Spirit of promise. *We are sealed in the body of Christ and the seal is the Holy Spirit of promise!*

Packages today are hermetically sealed, which means that air is drawn out of the package or the contents are protected from outside contamination. Nothing can get into the package and the only one who can break the seal is the one who redeems or buys the package.

Likewise, we are hermetically sealed in the body of Christ from any outside contamination. Nothing contaminating or corrupting or defiling, i.e. to our redemption by Jesus, can get inside the sealed body of Christ, and the only one who has a right to open the body of Christ is the Redeemer Himself, i.e. the one who promised to come back and redeem us. *He is coming again to redeem the package of His body, open it up, and pour us out in the New Jerusalem!*

Paul does not stop there, but gives more information concerning the Holy Spirit, in the next verse, which is really a continuation of the last verse. The word "given" is **not** in the Greek text. Verse 14 is just another phrase of the preceding sentence. The phrase is "who is a pledge of our inheritance." *The Holy Spirit was a pledge of, token of, or down payment on the Ephesians' final inheritance in Christ Jesus.*

Now, anybody knows that the greater the down payment, the greater the likelihood of the person returning to complete the transaction. Jesus left a great down payment, the gift of the Holy Spirit. The Holy Spirit was the down payment with a view towards the redemption of God's own possession. The Holy Spirit was given as a down payment towards God redeeming His own possession. And for what purpose? This was all to the praise of God's glory!

When Jesus, the Christ, left earth for glory, He left inside of us the precious down payment of the Holy Spirit. The down payment of the Holy Spirit says that Jesus is coming back again. Jesus is coming back again to redeem us; Jesus is coming back again to give us *an* inheritance; Jesus is coming back again to give us *our* inheritance in heaven.

How do we know that we have all of this in Christ? We know because of the presence of the indwelling Holy Spirit!!!

- I thank God for the Holy Spirit—He's my hermetically sealed Saran Wrap from the contamination of hell!
- I thank God for the Holy Spirit—He is the signature on my soul that identifies my owner.
- I thank God for the Holy Spirit—He is the down payment guaranteeing my inheritance in heaven.
- I thank God for the Holy Spirit—He is the down payment guaranteeing my redemption by Jesus Christ.

- I thank God for the Holy Spirit—He is the down payment that will <u>bring glory to God.</u>

We come now to the final verses we shall cover.

Do not grieve the Holy Spirit of God, by whom you were sealed for the day of redemption.

(Ephesians 4:30)

Be aware of the fact that it is possible to grieve the Holy Spirit of God, by whom we are sealed for the day of redemption. When we participate in sins of commission or omission, we grieve the heart of the Holy Spirit.

This is where we really begin to get into the relational principles of the Bible and the principles that drive my theology and my liveology. We tend to think of pleasing God in terms of **not** breaking His commandments. This kind of thinking has to do with:

- *rules* rather than *relationships*;
- *commandments* rather than *communion*;
- *objects* rather than *persons*;
- *legalism* rather than *love*; etc.

But here, in this verse of Scripture, Paul captures a *dynamic relational reality* between believers and the Holy Spirit. My BHAG (Big Hairy Audacious Goal), i.e. my miracle goal: "To change the world's concept of Christianity from reason-centered to relationship-centered!"

Most often, we tend to think of metaphors that are inanimate, which don't highlight relationships between living people. For instance: because of the Tylenol scare, most every product now has some type of seal. The seal often has a warning on it something to the effect of: "Do not use, if this seal is broken." This seal is *not to be broken* by anyone, except the purchaser. So, we think, "In God's grocery store, we are the product of God and the day of redemption is soon to come, when Jesus, the Christ, who paid for us through His shed blood, is coming to redeem us. But, until then, we are sealed, by the Holy Spirit!" **Now, while that is good, it falls far short of capturing the relational realities of the Christian life.** *We can't lose the sealing, but we can break the heart of the one who seals us for the day of redemption.*

Therefore, let's think of a biblical metaphor that has to do with living relationships. Think of the whole marriage system in the Jewish Culture. The Jewish custom of betrothal was somewhat like our engagement. Two Jewish families would agree to the marriage of their two children and the two would be betrothed. Betrothal was as binding as marriage, but it did not carry with it any conjugal rights. In this betrothal, the father of the prospective groom would arrange the marriage for His son. *The arrangement was sealed with a dowry, pledge, token, or down payment.* After this, the only thing that remained was the removal of the bride, by the groom, from the house of her father, to his own house. There seems to be literal truth in the Hebrew expression "to take a wife."

"After putting on festive dress, placing a 'garland' on his head, the bridegroom set forth from his house, attended by his groomsmen, preceded by a band of musicians or singers and accompanied by persons bearing lamps. Having reached the house of the bride, who with her companions anxiously expected his arrival, he conducted the whole party back to his own or his father's house, with every demonstration of gladness" (*New Unger's Bible Dictionary*).

On the honeymoon, the groom would check for a token of the bride's virginity. Now think of the heart of the groom, if he found out that his bride had been tampered with. His heart would be grieved! This exhortation is to the bride, "Don't grieve the heart of the one who will redeem you for all of eternity!"

Jesus has come from heaven to earth, to die on Calvary, to pay for us, His bride, through the shedding of His own precious blood. He left the down payment of the Holy Spirit and went back to heaven to prepare a place for us, so that where He is, there we may be also.

When He is ready to return, He will come with bright, shining glory and snatch us out of this world and take us back to the honeymoon suite, in His Father's house. *The seal is set! Our salvation can't be tampered with!*

But, while we are on that honeymoon, He will check for a token of our virginity, at the Bema Judgment seat. *Think of the grief that Jesus will experi-*

ence, if we have not been faithful to Him! Think of the grief we are going to experience, when we have to face our wounded lover!

But, in the meantime, we are waiting, but we are **not** waiting empty-handed. We have the dowry or the down payment of the *living* Holy Spirit in our hearts—right now!!!

On the other hand, unfortunately, the Spirit's grief does **not** await the return of Christ. His grief also starts right now.

So, don't grieve the heart of the Holy Spirit who is the dowry or down payment of the Father who has sealed us in Christ; 'till the day of redemption! "Forgive us Holy Spirit for grieving your heart! We love you and thank you for sealing us for the day of redemption!"

<u>Sealed</u>
- from contamination of hell
- says God is my owner
- my down pmt. m my father
- u u redemption
- for God's Glory
- Accountability

Chapter 7

The Controlling Work of the Holy Spirit

Now, we come to the controlling work of the Holy Spirit. This work of the Holy Spirit is probably best captured in:

> And do not get drunk with wine, for that is dissipation, but be filled with the Spirit.
>
> (Ephesians 5:18)

Before we can explore this very important ministry of the Holy Spirit, we have to explore the metaphor that Paul employs here, in which he contrasts being drunk on wine with being drunk in the Spirit. To get drunk on wine, I have to drink deeply of the wine.

Now, what happens when a person is **drunk with wine?** I have never been drunk, but from what I can observe, a person who is drunk with wine is **not** necessarily physically filled with wine, i.e. their stomachs may still have room in them, but the wine is influencing and literally **controlling** the behavior of that person.

When people are drunk with wine, the wine controls them and makes them different than they are normally or brings out aspects of them that are normally repressed.

- Quiet people may become loud.
- Shy people may become bold.
- Hard people may become gentle and reminiscent.
- Nasty people may become nice.

Wine controls or influences people to do things that they normally don't or cannot do in and of themselves! This is what it means to be filled with wine! *So, when I talk about this from now on, I am going to refer to this as being "controlled" by the Holy Spirit.* I am **not** going to use the term "filled," because that word does **not** convey to modern people the picture that Paul drew and because Luke also talks about being "filled" with the Holy Spirit, but means something different. This confuses people and confuses teaching, because we assume that Paul and Luke mean the same thing, when they use the word "filled." I am convinced the

Luke means something different than Paul, when he uses the word "filled," in Acts 2:4.

Now we can move forward and look at the contrasts and comparisons that Paul draws between being drunk with wine and being drunk in the Holy Spirit.

Paul gives a command to **not** get drunk with wine and then he describes the impact of being drunk with the words "in which is dissipation." The word "dissipation" is a very interesting word. The English word means "overindulgence in pursuit of pleasure" (*Microsoft Encarta World English Dictionary*). Isn't this exactly what drunkenness is all about? Many people are in such pain that they overindulge in alcoholic beverages, because they are in search of pleasure that will soothe the pain.

The Greek word is the negative of the word for "salvation." It is the word *asotia*, i.e. *sotia* made negative by the letter "a." Now the Greek word for "salvation" stands for:

- deliverance;
- healing;
- health;
- help;
- preservation;
- prosperity;
- rescue;
- safety;

- victory;
- welfare;

So, being drunk with wine is the opposite of what salvation stands for, i.e.:

- bondage instead of deliverance;
- sickness instead of healing;
- unhealthiness instead of health;
- burdens instead of help;
- spoilage instead of preservation;
- poverty instead of prosperity;
- abandonment instead of rescue;
- danger instead of safety;
- defeat instead of victory;
- calamity instead of welfare.

When a person is "filled" or "drunk" or "inebriated" with wine, that is dissipation, wasteful overindulgence, or literally "unsavedness."

As sinners in pain seek pleasure through overindulgence in alcoholic beverages, believers seek the Lord through deeply drinking in the Holy Spirit. Whether we are in pain or not, we should go to Jesus with everything, through being controlled by the Holy Spirit, and pleasure is a by-product of that control. *Being controlled by the Holy Spirit is "savedness"!*

In addition, this control of the Holy Spirit is compared to the control of wine, so the control of the Holy Spirit leads to:

- deliverance;
- healing;
- health;
- help;
- preservation;
- prosperity;
- rescue;
- safety;
- victory;
- welfare;

When we are controlled by the Holy Spirit we should be controlled in such a way that we are different than we normally are and demonstrating the fruit or characteristics of the Holy Spirit. We do **not** do this in and of ourselves, but the source of this power is the control of the indwelling Holy Spirit.

Let's get deeper into this metaphor by looking at the dynamic relationship between the believer and the Holy Spirit.

Please keep in mind that we are not containers or buckets, and the Holy Spirit is not liquid. We are persons and the Holy Spirit is a person who controls another person. *To be even more accurate, the Holy Spirit is Spirit and wants to control our spirits.* We are **not** discussing containers and liquids, but the dynamics of fellowship, within a relationship. *So, we are really talking about what it means, what it looks like, and the implications of the Person of the Holy Spirit controlling the person of a believer.*

Well, we know one thing from the beginning: when a person is controlled by wine, they tend to lose their balance, fall down, be foggy in their thinking, etc., etc., etc. By way of contrast, when a person is controlled by the Holy Spirit s/he gains spiritual balance, becomes more stable in his/her walk, has clarified thinking, etc., etc., etc.

In addition, as drunkenness seems crazy to others, so being controlled by the Holy Spirit may also seem crazy to others!

Now, we need to examine the text for more clues to what being controlled by the Spirit means, what it looks like, and when it begins.

Well, we can learn a great deal from the grammar of the words, "Be filled."

1. "Be filled" is in the imperative mood/mode, meaning it is a command.[30]

---

[30] E Stanley Ott, "Building One Another," A Letter of Encouragement, May, 1998, Volume X Number 4, The Holy Spirit, The Vital Churches Institute, Inc., Pittsburgh, Pennsylvania.

So, right off the bat, God commands us to be controlled by the Spirit. So, being controlled by the Holy Spirit is **not** optional for the believer, but mandatory. It is God's will that we are controlled by the Holy Spirit, and God never exhorts us to seek something He is **not** willing to provide! Consequently, God expects all believers to avoid being controlled with wine, in the same way that He expects all believers to be controlled by the Holy Spirit.

On the basis of this command, let us make up our minds to seek to be controlled by the Holy Spirit.

Jesus said, "You must be born again." Paul said, "Be filled with the Spirit." And in the next chapter, we shall consider a similar command recorded by Luke.

All right, let's look at the next clue with respect to Paul's use of "filling with the Spirit," which we have termed "the control of the Holy Spirit."

2. "Be filled" is in an instrumental sense.

The Word Biblical Commentary says, "The use of *en* with *plerousthai* in an instrumental sense is unusual."[31] This means that the Holy Spirit is the instrument of the filling. This indicates that "Believers are to be filled *by* the Spirit and thus

---

[31] Lincoln, Andrew T., *Word Biblical Commentary, Volume 42: Ephesians*, (Dallas, TX: Word Books, Publisher) 1998.

also filled *with* the Spirit."[32] The Commentary goes on to say, "Clearly, the Spirit mediates the fullness of God and of Christ to the believer."[33] *This is the fullness of the Spirit that should also exert His control over the believer!*

On to the next clue.

3. "Be filled" is a plural verb in the Greek, meaning "we" are all to be filled, i.e. every follower of Christ is to be filled.[34]

    So, do **not** limit this command to any particular group or subset of Christians. It is to all of us. No one is exempt! *God commands each follower and every follower of Jesus Christ to be controlled by the Holy Ghost.* Therefore, we must sincerely, diligently, and passionately seek the ongoing control of the Holy Spirit in our lives! Let's look at the next clue to what it means to be controlled by the Holy Spirit.

4. "Be filled" is in the present tense, meaning we are all to be filled with the Holy Spirit *right*

---

[32] Lincoln, Andrew T., *Word Biblical Commentary, Volume 42: Ephesians*, (Dallas, TX: Word Books, Publisher) 1998.

[33] Lincoln, Andrew T., *Word Biblical Commentary, Volume 42: Ephesians*, (Dallas, TX: Word Books, Publisher) 1998.

[34] E Stanley Ott, "Building One Another," A Letter of Encouragement, May, 1998, Volume X Number 4, The Holy Spirit, The Vital Churches Institute, Inc., Pittsburgh, Pennsylvania.

now and *every now to follow*, i.e. continuously in the present.[35]

We are not to be filled one time, but all the time. We are **not** to be filled in the past or in the future, but in ever present "now." We are to be filled every moment of every day. We are to be in a relationship and fellowship with the Holy Ghost where He is constantly controlling us! That's why I love the song.

I Need Thee Ev'ry Hour

I need Thee ev'ry hour,
Most gracious Lord;
No tender voice like Thine
Can peace afford.

REFRAIN

I need Thee, Oh, I need Thee;
Ev'ry hour I need Thee!
O bless me now, my Savior:
I come to Thee! Amen.

---

[35] E Stanley Ott, "Building One Another," A Letter of Encouragement, May, 1998, Volume X Number 4, The Holy Spirit, The Vital Churches Institute, Inc., Pittsburgh, Pennsylvania.

Then the Church of God in Christ saints extend the words of the refrain to:

> Every moment of the day, I need Thee;
> Every moment of the day, I need Thee!
> O bless me now, my Savior:
> I come to Thee! Amen.

The mode and tense of this verb also give us some insight into the timing of this ministry of the Holy Spirit.

The fact that the words "be filled" are in the imperative mode and the present tense means that he is commanding action that is to take place immediately and continuously. I want to be careful **not** to infer too much from the grammar, but it seems to me that Paul is commanding an action that should begin immediately and continue into the future. He did not use the *aorist*, which indicates a summary action that can be viewed as a snapshot, but the present tense which indicates an action that takes place now and should take place continuously. *I draw from this that every believer should seek to be continuously filled with the Holy Spirit, at some point in time, when they become aware of the teaching. Therefore, this takes place after Pentecost and usually after salvation.*

This brings up an interesting question, "Were people controlled by the Holy Spirit at

Pentecost?" The answer is, "It is possible, but that is **not** what Paul is talking about." "Were those on the Day of Pentecost controlled by the Holy Spirit at the moment that they were birthed into the Kingdom, baptized into the body of Christ, indwelled by the Spirit, and sealed with/ by the Spirit?" The answer is probably, "Yes," at least for that moment, but that is **not** what Paul is talking about. *Paul is not commanding people to be controlled by the Holy Spirit as an event on a specific day, but to be controlled by the Holy Spirit continuously, as a way of life. This control is for everyday living.*

I believe there is another way that Paul talks about this that will shed more light on the subject. Paul talks to the Galatians about "walking in the Spirit." He said:

> But I say, walk by the Spirit, and you will not carry out the desire of the flesh.
>
> (Galatians 5:16)

Walking in, by, or according to the Spirit is the same as being controlled by the Holy Spirit.

Therefore, we should seek to be controlled by the Holy Spirit so that we might walk according to the interests, mind, passions, and values, of the Holy Spirit!

So, the control of the Holy Spirit is for walking in the Spirit.

If people believe that they are controlled with the Holy Spirit upon salvation, I have **no** problem with that. They simply need to understand that the control of the Holy Spirit can be lost and needs to be continuously renewed. *We cannot stay drunk with wine, unless we continue to drink. Likewise, we cannot continue to be controlled by the Holy Spirit unless we continue to do those things that lead to being controlled by the Holy Spirit. What are those things? I will answer that question momentarily.*

But, the control of the indwelling Holy Spirit became available immediately after the Holy Spirit began to indwell people permanently, i.e. on the Great Day of Pentecost, and it remains available to all who seek that control, after they get saved.

Let's continue to explore this expansive command.

5. "Be filled" is in the passive voice.
   The passive voice means that something is being done to the subject. *Therefore, we are commanded to do something that is actually done to us.* This is a paradox that is only understood through the illuminating power of the Holy Ghost. There is one sense in which we are to take the initiative to be controlled by the Holy Spirit. I believe this

has a great deal to do with seeking that control. But, there is another sense in which the Holy Spirit takes the action to control us. *This would seem to suggest that although we have something to do with being filled with the Holy Ghost, we do not control this filling of the Holy Ghost.*

Now, what action should we take to be controlled by the Holy Spirit? Well, let me give you a list of things that we need to do:

1) Desire to be filled.
2) Seek the control of the Holy Spirit.
3) Ask for the control of the Holy Spirit.
4) Continually obey the Word of God.[36]
5) Continually repent concerning revealed sin.[37]
6) Receive this control by faith.
7) Yield to the control of the Holy Spirit. We become drunk with wine, when we yield to its control, by drinking more and more of it. We don't get drunk by reading the label on the bottle, but by drinking the contents. We become controlled by the Holy Spirit, when we yield to the Spirit. We don't become controlled by the

---

[36] R. A. Torrey, *The Baptism with the Holy Spirit*, Bethany House Publishers, Minneapolis, Minnesota, 1972, 43–44.
[37] R. A. Torrey, *The Baptism with the Holy Spirit*, Bethany House Publishers, Minneapolis, Minnesota, 1972, 41.

Spirit by simply reading the Bible, but by yielding to the One who reveals or illuminates the Word of God. We must give Him the right of way to control our spirits, souls, and bodies.

Now we must be aware of the fact that we can lose and regain the control of the Holy Spirit. How? Well, the control of the Holy Spirit is lost through sins of commission and omission.

So, we need to know what to do to continue to maintain the control of the Holy Spirit in our lives. Consequently, the action is twofold: first we need to keep short accounts with God; secondly the control of the Holy Spirit is maintained by the spiritual disciplines (*empowered by the indwelling Holy Spirit*), which is really practicing the presence of God. The spiritual disciplines are practices that have to do with cultivating intimacy with God. Those disciplines include, but are **not** limited to:

1) Prayer.
2) Meditation.
3) Bible Study.
4) Fasting.
5) Simplicity.
6) Silence.
7) Solitude.

8)   Frugality.

9)   Giving.

10) Submission.

11) Chastity.

12) Secrecy or modesty.

13) Sacrifice.

14) Service.

15) Confession (Grief).

16) Worship.

17) Fellowship.

18) Celebration.

Thank You Lord for the opportunity to be controlled by Your Spirit, in our everyday lives!

Chapter 8

The Empowering Work of the Holy Spirit

A preacher named George Duncan once went to visit some friends in the English countryside. For years they had lived in an old-fashioned, run-down building. To Mr. Duncan's surprise, he discovered that the house had been completely remodeled. The people had installed new lights, an electric stove, and many other pieces of modern equipment. But, he was even more surprised to see the lady of the house still using a kerosene stove for cooking and oil lamps for lighting. After greeting him, she said, "George, don't look so confused. We've had a great change here, but we just haven't turned on the power yet."

Well, this ministry of the Holy Spirit is about turning the power on in our lives! We come, finally, to the last ministry of the Holy Spirit, in the life of the sinner-believer, which is the empowering work of the Holy Spirit.

This work of the Holy Spirit is probably best captured in Acts 1:5, Acts 2:4, and Acts 11:16.

> For John baptized with water, but you will be baptized with the Holy Spirit not many days from now.
>
> (Acts 1:5)

> And they were all filled with the Holy Spirit and began to speak with other tongues, as the Spirit was giving them utterance.
>
> (Acts 2:4)

> And I remembered the word of the Lord, how He used to say, "John baptized with water, but you will be baptized with the Holy Spirit."
>
> (Acts 11:16)

Since Acts 11:16 is a reference back to Acts 1:5, we shall only deal with the first two Scriptures. Let's begin with the first Scripture. When dealing with the Bible, it is important to take into consideration the context of the verses one is studying. Although we have done this all along, we have not printed some of the texts in this book, because of space. Nevertheless, because of the importance and size of this text, allow me to do so now.

The first account I composed, Theophilus, about all that Jesus began to do and teach, until the day when He was taken up to heaven, after He had by the Holy Spirit given orders to the apostles whom He had chosen. To these He also presented Himself alive after His suffering, by many convincing proofs, appearing to them over a period of forty days and speaking of the things concerning the kingdom of God. Gathering them together, He commanded them not to leave Jerusalem, but to wait for what the Father had promised, "Which," He said, "you heard of from Me; for John baptized with water, but you will be baptized with the Holy Spirit not many days from now."

(Acts 1:1–5)

Luke is recapitulating and rehearsing the history of the early Church for Theophilus. He begins by reminding Theophilus of the first account. The first account was the Gospel of Luke. Luke is now continuing what he began in the Gospel of Luke, here in the Acts of the Apostles, which I like to think of more as "The Acts of the Holy Spirit."

In the first account, that is the Gospel of Luke, Luke covered Christ's conception, birth, life, and all that He began to do and teach, until the ascension, i.e. the day that He was taken up to heaven.

Jesus was taken up to heaven after He had, by the Holy Spirit, given orders to the apostles whom He had chosen. The orders were the commission that Jesus gave to His disciples, before He ascended. This commission is recorded in Matthew 28:16–20; Mark 16:15–18; Luke 24:44–49; John 20:21–23; and 1 Corinthians 15:6.

To these same apostles, Jesus presented Himself alive, after His suffering, by many convincing proofs. These proofs included many post-resurrection appearances. Jesus appeared to the apostles, and to others, over a period of forty days, and talked about things concerning the Kingdom of God.

Now we come to the verses that have to do with the empowering work of the Holy Spirit.

In verse four, Luke rehearses the story of how Jesus gathered the apostles together and commanded them **not** to leave Jerusalem, but to wait for what the Father had promised, "Which," Jesus said to the apostles, "you have heard of from me; for John baptized with water, but you will be baptized with the Holy Spirit not many days from now."

First, what was the promise of the Father, which they had heard of from Jesus. Well, this is a reference back to:

> And behold, I am sending forth the promise of My Father upon you; but you are to stay in the city until you are clothed with power from on high.
>
> (Luke 24:49)

I cannot take the time to take you through all of the study that I did on this topic, so let it suffice to say that the promise of the Father is the promise of the gift of the

Holy Spirit, that was first given to Abraham in the promise of his *seed*, and extends through history to the birth, death, burial, resurrection, and present mystery reign of Jesus Christ, who began to fulfill the promise by sending the Comforter.

Even though I won't take the time and space to give you my whole study of this subject, Jesus gives us a synonym for the promise of the Father, which is very descriptive. The synonym is in the command, ". . . but you are to stay in the city until you are clothed with power from on high." *So, whatever the promise of the Father is, it will result in being clothed with power from on high.*

Christ's command here captures the absolute indispensability of the "Lukan" filling of the Holy Spirit. Because "the promise of the Father" is a synonym used by Luke for "the filling in the Holy Spirit," this is a command related to power of service, which is of similar importance and intensity to "you must be born again," with respect to salvation, and "Be filled with the Spirit," with respect to power for living."

Now we can return to Acts 1:5.

> For John baptized with water, but you will be baptized with the Holy Spirit not many days from now.
>
> (Acts 1:5)

These are the words of Jesus informing his apostles, and their companions, of the coming baptizing work of the Holy Spirit. I must digress for a moment. This is another synonym, used by Luke, to talk about the "Lukan" filling of the Holy Spirit. As you read through the Gospel of Luke and the book of Acts, you will see that a number of synonyms are employed by Luke for the same experience. I believe Luke did this to reference the various aspects of this marvelous work of the Holy Spirit. All right, back to the subject. This baptizing, "filling," or *empowering* work of the Holy Spirit would begin **not** many days from His prophecy. In actuality, it would be exactly ten days in the future, on The Great Day of Pentecost, when they would all be baptized by, with, or *in* the Holy Spirit. *And, according to Luke 24:49, this baptism would clothe them with power!*

I pray that this is enough for us to begin to see that this is the empowering ministry of the Holy Spirit and it began on the Great Day of Pentecost.

Let me clearly state that:

- This is **not** what Paul is talking about in 1 Corinthians 12:13. There Paul talked about *believing-sinners* being baptized into the sphere of the body of Christ, through the Holy Spirit. The result is that these believers become members of the body of Christ. *That is what we called the baptizing work of the Holy Spirit.*
- This is **not** what Paul talked about in Ephesians 5:18. There Paul talked about *believers* being controlled by the Holy Spirit, for everyday liv-

ing. *This is what we called the controlling work of the Holy Spirit.*

In contradistinction, here Luke is talking about *apostles and believers* of Jesus Christ being baptized into the sphere of the Holy Spirit, by Jesus Christ, for the purpose of being clothed with power from on high. *But, we don't know the purpose of this power yet!*

Well, we can gain even more information, when we look at Christ's words explaining the baptism in the Holy Spirit. All we have to do is keep reading. Notice the following verses:

> So when they had come together, they were asking Him, saying, "Lord, is it at this time You are restoring the kingdom to Israel?" He said to them, "It is not for you to know times or epochs which the Father has fixed by His own authority; but you will receive power when the Holy Spirit has come upon you; and you shall be My witnesses both in Jerusalem, and in all Judea and Samaria, and even to the remotest part of the earth."
>
> (Acts 1:6–8)

In this short passage of Scripture, Jesus talks more about the power that He mentioned in Luke 24:49. Here He explains the purpose of the power of the Holy Spirit. *The power of the Holy Spirit would make them witnesses in Jerusalem, Judea, Samaria, and the remotest parts of the earth.* The baptism in the Holy Spirit would empower the apostles and their companions to be witnesses of Jesus Christ and to transact Kingdom business. A survey of the book of Acts, shows that the apostles and their companions operated in *miracles, signs, and wonders,* when they were transacting Kingdom business. *This, again, is the empowering ministry of the Holy Spirit!*

All of this comes to a head in Acts 2:4, which is the fulfillment of Acts 1:5. To get the gist of this fulfillment, we read:

> When the day of Pentecost had come, they were all together in one place. And suddenly there came from heaven a noise like a violent rushing wind, and it filled the whole house where they were sitting. And there appeared to them tongues as of fire distributing themselves, and they rested on each one of them. And they were all filled with the Holy Spirit and began to speak with other tongues, as the Spirit was giving them utterance.
>
> (Acts 2:1–4)

The Day of Pentecost was an annual feast, but this particular celebration was like no other, so I refer to this New Testament Dispensational watershed day as "The Great Day of Pentecost." On the Great Day of Pentecost, when all of the apostles and their companions had gathered together in one place, in Jerusalem, to wait as Jesus had commanded them, the promise of the Father was poured out. *Suddenly there came from heaven a noise like a violent rushing wind, which filled the house where they were sitting.* And there appeared visible tongues of fire that seemed to distribute themselves among them and sit on each one of their heads. And they were all "filled" with the Holy Spirit and began to speak with human languages that they had never learned, as the Spirit was giving them to speak forth.

We are only centering on the terminology "filled with the Holy Spirit." First of all, let me say that it is obvious that what Luke recorded here is the fulfillment of what Jesus promised in Luke 24:49, Acts 1:5, and Acts 1:8. *Therefore, we know that being "filled" with the Holy Spirit is the same thing as being "baptized in the Holy Spirit," which is the same thing as "being clothed with power from on high," which is the same thing as "the promise of the Father." This is the same author, using similar words, discussing the same subject.* Hence, when Luke uses these terms they are *dynamic synonyms* for the same thing. The synonyms are dynamic in that they each communicate a different aspect concerning the experience of the "Lukan" filling in the Holy Spirit.

In the Gospel of Luke and the book of Acts, Luke uses the following dynamic synonyms for the empowering work of the Holy Spirit:

- Being clothed with power from on high;
- The promise of the Father;
- The baptism *in* the Holy Spirit;

- The coming of the Holy Spirit upon people;
- The filling of the Holy Spirit;
- The pouring forth of the Holy Spirit;
- The promise of the Spirit;
- The gift of the Holy Spirit;
- The falling of the Holy Spirit upon people;
- The gift of the Holy Spirit being poured out on people; and
- Received the Holy Spirit.

Once again, this also means that when Luke used the terminology "filled with the Holy Spirit" he does not mean the same thing as Paul. That is why I called what Paul talked about in Ephesians 5:18 "the controlling ministry of the Holy Spirit," and I am calling what Luke is talking about here "the empowering ministry of the Holy Spirit." If I would use any other terms for this event, I would tend to call it "the baptism in the Holy Spirit" or the "Lukan" filling of the Holy Spirit.

As I have taught this to others, they seem to be confused, probably because of the newness of the paradigm and the nomenclature, so let me review what I just gave you.

- Ephesians 5:18 is *the controlling work* of the Holy Spirit or the "Pauline" filling of the Holy Spirit.

- Luke 24:49, Acts 1:8, and Acts 2:4 are *the empowering work* of the Holy Spirit or the "Lukan" filling of the Holy Spirit.

There are many contrasts between the two, but that must await another book.

Before we move on, please note that Stronstad points out, in *The Charismatic Theology of Luke*, that Luke uses the terminology "baptized in the Spirit" three times, while Paul only uses it once, and even then Paul's terminology is different. Paul said, "by one Spirit we are all baptized into one body." Yet, Paul's theology defines the terminology. Likewise, the terminology "filled with the Spirit" occurs nine times in Luke's writings and only one time in Paul's writings, yet, again, Paul's theology defines the terminology. *I submit to you that this is wrong. It is what I call "Pauliolatry" and it should be reconsidered.*

Luke was a theologian and historian in his own right and he was writing about a different experience than Paul. Let's let Luke stand on his own two theological and historical feet!

Please don't interpret me as having any problem with or bias against Paul. Paul was a brilliant and important figure in the early Church, who has penned for us most of the New Testament. Nevertheless, this does not mean that every writer and text in the New Testament should be only interpreted through Paul's theology.

Consequently, I am going to refer to this ministry of the Holy Spirit either as "baptized in the Holy Spirit," or "The 'Lukan" filling in the Holy Spirit," or "the empowering ministry" of the Holy Spirit.

Now, let's talk a little bit about the empowering ministry of the Holy Spirit.

- Remember that the Great Day of Pentecost is the dispensational divide that ushers in a whole new dispensation, dynamic, and dimension of the Holy Spirit.
- Remember that the Great Day of Pentecost is the birthday of the New Testament Church.
- Remember that the Great Day of Pentecost is the initiation of at least five works of the Holy Spirit in the life of the sinner-believer.

It is important to point out that Luke's filling of the Holy Spirit was an experience for empowering believers to be witnesses and to transact Kingdom business. This was not just to *do* witnessing, but also to *be* a witness, and transact Kingdom business that includes healing the sick, binding up broken hearts, building up the church, and anything that ushers in the Kingdom of God. *The controlling ministry of the Holy Spirit is for walking in the Spirit. The Empowering ministry of the Holy Spirit is for witnessing, warring, and worshipping in the Spirit, i.e. service.*

Let me give you an illustration. In America, we have the right to bear arms. Some of us may have a .22 calibur or some other small handgun to protect ourselves. That is fine, when you are walking around, in your everyday life, but if you were enlisted in the army and sent to the battlefield of a war, your .22 calibur would not be the proper weapon. The weaponry on today's battlefield is not only different; it is more powerful. The control of the Holy Spirit is for use in our everyday walk with the Lord. The empowering of the Holy Spirit is for witnessing, worshipping, and warring in the Spirit, against the enemy.

Now, while most of the other works of the Holy Spirit involve a state, condition, or position, which the believer may not be aware of, the empowering ministry of the Spirit involves a dynamic experience. This work of the Holy Spirit is experienced in a dynamic way. None who received the empowering ministry of the Holy Spirit, in the Bible, were unaware of the experience. They may **not** have known exactly what happened to them, but they knew that something very dynamic had happened to them.

Also keep in mind that Luke's perspective of the Holy Spirit is Charismatic and not soteriological. When we say Charismatic, in this context, we mean the perspective that "God's gift of His Spirit to His servants, either individually or collectively, is to anoint, empower, or inspire them for divine service. As recorded in the Scripture . . . this charismatic activity is necessarily an experiential phenomenon."[38] The term soteriological comes from the

---

[38] Roger Stronstad, *The Charismatic Theology of St. Luke*, Hendrickson Publishers, Inc., Peabody Massachusetts, 1984, 13.

Greek word *soteria*, which means "salvation." *So, the empowering ministry has to do with power for service, not salvation!*

We need teaching concerning the convicting work of the Holy Spirit, the birthing work of the Holy Spirit, the baptizing work of the Holy Spirit, the indwelling work of the Holy Spirit, and the sealing work of the Holy Spirit, because they are more positional than experiential. But, we also need teaching concerning the empowering work of the Holy Spirit, so that we might understand what we can experience and the purpose of this experience.

There are going to be some who don't agree with this and can't accept it. That's fine, because it is **not** about salvation—but service! If my conclusions are right, opponents will simply not accept a gift/manifestation and specific power that is available to them.

All right, let's move on to the next observation.

Every believer in the upper room received the experience. This empowering ministry of the Holy Spirit is for every believer, **not** just *special* believers. Although many modern believers are **not** receiving this empowering ministry of the Holy Spirit, it was experienced by every believer in the upper room and remains available today. Peter said:

> For the promise is for you and your children and for all who are far off, as many as the Lord our God will call to Himself.
>
> (Acts 2:39)

Do you want this empowering of the Holy Spirit? It is available for you today!

But how do we receive this empowering ministry of the Holy Spirit? Well, there is a clue in Christ's words:

> If you then, being evil, know how to give good gifts to your children, how much more will your heavenly Father give the Holy Spirit to those who ask Him?
> (Luke 11:13)

Now, we don't have to ask the Lord for the convicting work of the Holy Spirit, or birthing work of the Holy Spirit, or the baptizing work of the Holy Spirit, or indwelling work of the Holy Spirit, or the sealing work of the Holy Spirit, because they come automatically with salvation. But, if we want to be empowered to witness and transact Kingdom business, in this present dispensation, we need to ask God for this gift of the Holy Spirit, who will clothe us with power from on high.

For those who are more scholarly, who believe in a "Q" document, which was used by Matthew and Luke. Luke obviously went out of his way to amend Q. Matthew asks, in Matthew 7:11, ". . . how much more will your heavenly Father give what is **good** to those who ask" (*emphasis mine*); but Luke says, ". . . how much more will your heavenly Father give the **Holy Spirit** to those who ask Him" (*emphasis mine*).

In addition, once we ask for this empowering of the Holy Spirit, we need to receive God's gift. *One of the best ways to receive this gift is to tell God, "Thank You!"*

All right, let's move to the next observation.

Although there were certain criteria that needed to be met before this experience was given, these criteria did **not** seem to be *conditional* as much as they were *preparatory*, i.e. they were in Jerusalem as Jesus commanded, they were all together in one place, there was probably an atmosphere of prayer, etc. Yet, the Holy Spirit seemed to have come—on schedule—on the Great Day of Pentecost.

Although we won't take the time to explore this, we can tell from Acts 4:31 that the experience is repeatable. There they prayed; the place where they had gathered was shaken; they were all filled with the Holy Spirit; and they began to speak the Word of God with boldness. Please note that there were **no** tongues mentioned here, but there was the *inspired speaking* of the Word of God with freedom, confidence, or boldness. Remember: Paul also uses the word "filled," but for the controlling ministry of the Holy Spirit!

From the Great Day of Pentecost until now, the empowering ministry of the Holy Spirit has been and continues to be an available, repeatable experience to all believers for the purpose of being witnesses and transacting Kingdom business, which—in Luke–Acts is accompanied by some type of inspired speech, and that inspired speech tended to be tongues and/or prophecy.

Even though some kind of inspired speech accompanied the empowering ministry of the Holy Spirit in each instance, in Luke–Acts, and that speech tended to be tongues and/or prophecy, I do not teach that any of this is evidentiary, because I have **no** command that says, "You must have inspired speech, or tongues, or prophecy to receive the empowering ministry of the Holy Spirit." Nevertheless, from the text of Luke-Acts, I have drawn the conclusion that we should expect some kind of inspired speech, when we are "empowered by the Holy Spirit" for service.

Although cessationists teach that the manifestations of the Spirit in 1 Corinthians 12:8–10 have ceased, according to their interpretation of what Paul means by "the perfect" (1 Corinthians 13:10), many of them seem to be backing away from that teaching. This is wise, in light of the fact that most scholars interpret "the perfect" as the Second Coming of Jesus, the Christ, not the completion of the canon of the Bible.

On the contrary, every time that we need power to witness, or to transact Kingdom business, all that we need to do is pray and receive this ministry of the Spirit and Kingdom power, and expect God to speak and act through us.

According to Luke 24:49, this empowering is absolutely necessary to witnessing, because Jesus commanded the apostles to go to Jerusalem and wait for the promise of the Father. This is a divine enablement for service given sovereignly or specifically to believers who ask for it, seek for it, or are ready to receive it. *Just like the American Express Card—"Don't leave home without it!" Although this command is not as direct as Paul's "be filled with the Spirit" (Ephesians 5:18), it amounts to the same thing.*

When you study all of the other recorded occurrences of the empowering of the Holy Spirit, it seems that this empowering is subsequent to or after salvation. *It is very much like the Holy Spirit coming upon Old Testament saints for service, except that the New Testament empowering is available to all believers, for the asking.*

God evidently intended to create an empowered community of empowered people to participate in the Mystery Kingdom and to usher in the Messianic Kingdom, i.e. the final manifestation of the Kingdom. Therefore, it is time for those of us who believe in the empowering ministry of the Holy Spirit to come out of the closet of shame and into the spotlight of the biblical respectability.

For those of you who are interested in continuing to study and understand the differences in these works of the Holy Spirit in the life of the sinner-believer, following are three charts to help you understand what may seem to be confusing works of the Holy Spirit, and a theological position paper to give a little more clarity.

I thank God for the empowering work of the Holy Spirit.

Comparing the Confusing Works of the Holy Spirit			
The Birthing Work of the Holy Spirit	The Baptizing Work of the Holy Spirit	The Controlling Work of the Holy Spirit	The Empowering Work of the Holy Spirit
John 3:1-8	1 Corinthians 12:12-13	Ephesians 5:18	Luke 24:49; Acts 1:5; 2:4; 11:16
Born of the Spirit	Baptized into the body of Christ	"Paul's" filled with the Spirit	Clothed with power from on high; baptized in the Holy Spirit; "Luke's" filled with the Spirit
Occurs at salvation	Occurs at salvation	Occurs after salvation	Occurs after salvation
More positional than experiential	More positional than experiential	A Condition	An Experience
The position establishes citizenship in the kingdom of God.	The position establishes membership in the body of Christ.	The condition is for power to live the Christian life.	The experience is for power to witness and transact kingdom business.
Non-repeatable	Non-repeatable	Sustainable	Repeatable
A child of the King	A brother, sister, or fellow heir with Christ	A Spirit-controlled pilgrim, sojourner, or traveler	A Spirit-empowered witness

The Eight Ministries of the Holy Spirit

A finished work	A finished work	Walking in the Spirit (*Galatians 5:16-26*)	Witnessing, worshipping, and warring in the Spirit [Kingdom business] (*Acts 1:8; 2:11; Mark 16:17*)

	Salvation *Versus* The Empowering Work of the Holy Spirit	
Operation	Salvation (*Romans 10:8-10*)	The Empowering Work of the Holy Spirit (*The most common name used by Luke is the "filling" with the Holy Spirit*) (*Luke 1:15, 41, 67; Acts 2:4; 4:8, 31; 9:17; 13:9, 52*)
Terminology	Saved; adopted into the body of Christ; belief in Jesus Christ; born of the Spirit; born from above, the new birth, faith in Jesus Christ; repentance towards God; justification by faith; forgiveness of sins; reconciled to God; redeemed; etc.	The filling of the Holy Spirit; received the Holy Spirit; full of the Holy Spirit; the promise of the Father; being clothed with power from on high; the baptism in the Holy Spirit; the coming of the Holy Spirit upon people; the pouring forth of the Holy Spirit; the promise of the Spirit; the gift of the Holy Spirit; the falling of the Holy Spirit upon people; the gift of the Holy Spirit being poured out.

The Eight Ministries of the Holy Spirit

Works of the Spirit	The drawing, convicting, birthing, baptizing, indwelling, sealing works	Empowering (*the controlling work is usually co-relational, i.e. they tend to be found together*)
Timing	At salvation (*except the drawing and convicting work of the Holy Spirit, which may be just prior to salvation, i.e. in logical order*)	After salvation
Permanence	At once and once and for all (*1 Corinthians 6:19*)	The initial experience is at once and once and for all, while the filling seems to be repeatable as needed for witnessing and kingdom work (*Acts 4:31*)
Command	John 3:1-6; Acts 16:30-31	Luke 24:49; Acts 1:4-5
Promise	Romans 10:13	Acts 2:39
Purpose	Eternal salvation	Empowering for witnessing and transacting kingdom business (*for operating in the Mystery Kingdom to usher in the Messianic Kingdom*)
Condition	Faith (*Romans 10:13*)	Asking, seeking, knocking, and receiving (*Luke 11:13*)

Positional Versus Experiential	More positional than experiential—New Creation	More experiential than positional—New Power
Gifting	Bestows the gifts of Romans 12:3-8 and offices of Ephesians 4:7-13	Bestows the capacity for the manifestations of 1 Corinthians 12:8-10
Relationship to Peace	The Peace of God (*Romans 5:1*)	Peace With God (*Philippians 4:7*)
Biblical Typology	The Exodus out of Egypt (*Crossing the Red Sea*)	Entrance into the Promised Land (*Crossing the Jordan River*)

Chart Three

The Controlling Work of the Holy Spirit *Versus* The Empowering Work of the Holy Spirit	
The Controlling Work of the Holy Spirit	**The Empowering Work of the Holy Spirit**
Taught by Paul in Ephesians 5:18	Taught by Luke in Luke 24:49; Acts 1:5, 8; 2:4
Called "filled with the Holy Spirit" one time in Ephesians 5:18	Called "filled with the Holy Spirit" nine times in Luke 1:15, 41, 67; Acts 2:4; 4:8, 31; 9:17; 13:9, 52
A synonym for a state (*the state or condition is metaphorized as being drunk or controlled by wine—hence the choice of the terminology "the control of the Holy Spirit"*)	A synonym for an experience (*The filling of the Holy Spirit; received the Holy Spirit; the promise of the Father; being clothed with power from on high; the baptism in the Holy Spirit; the coming of the Holy Spirit upon people; the pouring forth of the Holy Spirit; the promise of the Spirit; the gift of the Holy Spirit; the falling of the Holy Spirit upon people; the gift of the Holy Spirit being poured out*)
The state that is captured in the literal translation "be filled now and every now thereafter," is for power to live the Christian life	The experience is for power to be a witness of Jesus, the Christ, and to transact Kingdom business (*which often includes miracles, signs, and wonders*)

The Eight Ministries of the Holy Spirit

The state tends to be manifested in encouraging one another, singing and making melody in our hearts to God, an attitude of thankfulness, and being subject to one another (*Ephesians 5:18-20*)	The experience is accompanied by inspired speech, in Luke–Acts (*tongues, prophecy, preaching the Word with power*), and the inspired speech tends to be tongues and/or prophecy
Maintained by the spiritual disciplines (*empowered by the indwelling Holy Spirit*)	A divine enablement for service given sovereignly or to believers who ask, seek for it, or are ready to receive (*the right condition through various methods, i.e. prayer, laying on of hands, listening to preaching, etc.*) (*"the filling of the Holy Spirit" in the passive voice; "the receiving of the Holy Spirit" in the active voice"*)
The state is to be continual	The experience is repeatable
Tends to release the spiritual gifts of Romans 12:3-8 and gifts or offices of Ephesians 4:7-13 and (The word "gifts" is *5486 charisma* "in the technical Pauline sense *Charismata* denote extraordinary powers, distinguishing certain Christians and enabling them to service Christ, the reception of which is due to the power of divine grace operating in their souls by the Holy Spirit" (*Thayer's Greek English Lexicon*).	Bestows and empowers the capacity for the spiritual manifestations of 1 Corinthians 12:8-10 (*The word "manifestation" is a very important word. It is the word **phanerosis**. This word means a disclosure, announcement, evidencing, a making known, revelation. "The basic Greek root **phan** is the same as that for an apparition or ghost. Hence, it can have overtones of a disclosure that sort of 'flashes forth.' It is used in this context as a synonym for 'gift,' but with the apparent nuance that these nine aspects can 'flash forth from any believer as needed' ['for the profit of all']).*"[39]

[39] Jack W. Hayford, *People of the Spirit*, Thomas Nelson Publishers, Nashville, Tennessee, 1993, 80.

	"They are not necessarily 'resident' gifts . . . but rather spontaneously granted tools given as the need arises and the Spirit determines (1 Corinthians 12:11)."[40] *"Thus each 'gift' is a 'manifestation,' a disclosure of the Spirit's activity in their midst."*[41])
Has to do with the Fruit of the Spirit (*Galatians 5:22-23*)	Has to do with the manifestations of the Spirit (*1 Corinthians 12:8-10*)
Walking in the Spirit (*Galatians 5:16-26*)	Witnessing, worshipping, and warring in the Spirit (*Acts 1:8; 2:11; Mark 16:17*)
Co-relational with the empowering work of the Holy Spirit	Co-relational with the controlling work of the Holy Spirit

[40] Jack W. Hayford, *People of the Spirit*, Thomas Nelson Publishers, Nashville, Tennessee, 1993, 111.

[41] Gordon D. Fee, *The First Epistle to the Corinthians*, William B. Eerdmans Publishing Company, Grand Rapids, Michigan, 1987, 589.

Epilogue: Towards a Biblecostal™ Theology and Hermeneutic

(Revised 06/26/2004)
Bishop Joey Johnson

I am continuing to develop a biblical theology and hermeneutic for what I call "Biblecostalism™." I coined the term "Biblecostal™" on October 16, 1998, in an attempt to keep from being theologically categorized and lumped in with people who are different from us—not because of any sense of superiority or pride, but for the sake of clarity in teaching. There are two seemingly opposite poles of theological teaching. I refer to them as Pentecostal and Fundamental or Conservative Evangelical, with the latter having its roots in Fundamentalism. I want to state for the record that I object to the terms and the stereotypes attached to the terms Pentecostal, Fundamental, and Evangelical, as they are currently being used. In a manner of speaking we are all Pentecostal, because the Church was born on the Great Day of Pentecost. We are all Fundamental, if we believe in the fundamentals of the Bible. We are all Evangelicals, if we believe in the Evangel, i.e. the Gospel of Jesus Christ. Nevertheless, these names are commonly used in America with some sense of meaning. So, I will reluctantly use them as they are currently used.

One of the distinctive characteristics of Biblecostalism™ is that we hold to some of the beliefs of both Pentecostalism and Evangelicalism simultaneously, while leaning towards some of the distinctives of Pentecostalism with respect to the Luke's perspective of "the baptism in the Holy Spirit" (Luke 1:5) or "filling" with the Holy Spirit (Luke 2:4). I call this the empowering ministry of the Holy Spirit. Like the Bible and the post-postmodern world in which we live, it is no longer inconceivable to hold to two beliefs or positions that seem to be antithetical. It is now possible to be both/and, rather than either/or.

We are not classically Pentecostal, because we do not hold to the view that the "initial evidence" of the contemporary baptism in the Holy Spirit or empowering ministry of the Holy Spirit is speaking in tongues. Although I believe I understand those who teach this doctrine, agree that a good case can be made for this teaching, and believe that tongues are likely to occur in conjunction with the empowering ministry of the Holy Spirit, we do not teach evidentiary tongues because 1) there is **no** direct biblical statement that speaking in tongues is the "evidence" of the baptism in the Holy Ghost, 2) although a case for this teaching can be built from the texts involved, speaking in tongues is not stated in every occurrence of the baptism in the Holy Spirit, 3) although the "initial evidence" doctrine captures the expectation of the texts involved, "The focus on evidence can lead to a preoccupation with a single crisis experience. Evidentiary tongues can also be readily confused with a badge of holiness, an experience that signifies that one has entered into a higher degree of spiritual maturity."[42]

While not all those who hold to a baptism in the Holy Spirit that is subsequent to salvation would hold to the "initial evidence" doctrine, this is nonetheless widely held to represent Pentecostalism.

We are Evangelical, but more, because we agree with many of the teachings of Evangelicals with the major exception of their take on the baptism in the Holy Spirit and their belief that the manifestations of the Spirit, listed in 1 Corinthians 12:8–10, are no longer in operation.

We might be called "Charismatic," but the Charismatic Renewal Movement was a movement within main-

---

[42] William and Robert Menzies, Spirit and Power: Foundations of Pentecostal Experience, Zondervan Publishing House, Grand Rapids, Michigan, 2000, 143.

line denominations, and we are nondenominational or transdenominational.

Furthermore, we cannot be classified as "the Third Wave," which describes the intrusion and belief in the manifestations of the Spirit within the confines of conservative Evangelicalism. While making room for Pentecostal manifestations of the Spirit, this group still holds to the Evangelical view of the baptism in the Holy Spirit. In light of these differences, it seems better to come up with our own designation.

During the course of this paper, I will make some critical observations about both Classical Pentecostals and Classical Conservative Evangelicals. I do not do so with any sense of ultimate judgment, animosity, or superiority, but only to point out differences for the purpose of understanding. This is one of the teaching methods of Jesus, who often taught by contrast. Undoubtedly, few people live at these extremes, but are probably somewhere in the middle. Nevertheless, understanding something about these extremes can help us understand the controversy.

I am **not** at this time commenting upon the Charismatic movement in mainline churches known as Neo-Pentecostalism or the Third Wave. What I am developing is a fresh theology and a hermeneutic. Theology is basically the study of God, and I am developing a written, systematic theology of what we believe the Bible teaches with respect to the empowering ministry of the Holy Spirit. The word "hermeneutic" has to do with Bible interpretation. I am also developing our "hermeneutic" or the way we tend to interpret the Bible and certain critical passages with respect to the empowering ministry of the Holy Spirit today.

After going back into the Word of God and restudying these things, over the last seven years, I believe I am coming to some conclusions. But, I can make no final statement or teaching, because the depths of the Word of God can never be fully or finally plumbed. We believe in what the Reformers referred to as *semper reformonda*, i.e. always reforming. Therefore, this is necessarily a work in progress.

It is important to develop a theology and a hermeneutic, because both are involved in understanding this controversial subject. To get a better perspective of this whole discussion, we need to explore some of the history behind it. Donald W. Dayton, in his book *Theological Roots of Pentecostalism*, cites a divide between the Pentecostal and the conservative Evangelical hermeneutic in the mid-1800s. Developing Pentecostals, of that era, seemed to rely upon a Lukan, historical narrative hermeneutic, while developing conservative Evangelicals, of that era, seemed to rely upon a Pauline, didactic hermeneutic.[43] This is only one explanation of an ongoing dichotomy that I see between Classical Pentecostals and Classical Conservative Evangelicals.

---

[43] Donald W. Dayton, *Theological Roots of Pentecostalism*, Scarecrow Press, Metuchen, New Jersey, 1987, 23.

A dichotomy that may be captured in the question, "Can there be a Pentecostal scholar?"

Classical Pentecostals seem to place an emphasis upon experience, with less grounding of that experience in the Bible. Conservative Evangelicals seem to put an emphasis upon the Aristotelian logic of systematic, propositional theology, with little room for genuine personal experiences and the interpretation of the genuine experiences of the book of Acts. There is a dichotomy between emphasis upon the historical, narrative texts of Luke and Acts and the didactic epistles of the Apostle Paul. Again, historian and scholar, Donald Dayton says, "Narrative texts are notoriously difficult to interpret theologically." In addition, Reformed theologian, R. C. Sproul, said in the tape series "Knowing Scripture," "Do not draw conclusions from narratives only." Before going forward, I want to point out that both Pentecostals and Evangelicals draw conclusions from narratives only, when it suits their purposes.

All right, let's return to Dayton's words. Some Classical "Pentecostals read the accounts of Pentecost in Acts and insist that the general pattern of the early Church's reception of the Spirit, especially as it is in some sense separated in time from the Church's experience of Jesus, must be replicated in the life of each individual believer.

In making this claim, Pentecostalism stands in a long tradition of a 'subjectivizing hermeneutic.'"[44] Yet,

---

[44] Donald W. Dayton, *Theological Roots of Pentecostalism*, Scarecrow Press, Metuchen, New Jersey, 1987, 23.

I state, on the contrary, that this statement does not prove that narrative passages can never be used to determine doctrine, and that it is done often. I agree that doctrinal statements should be in keeping with the teaching of the entire Bible, but specific doctrines are drawn from both didactic texts and narratives.

Finally, I have found at least one book that presents the Pentecostal perspective from a scholarly, biblical perspective. It is *Spirit and Power,* by William and Robert Menzies. The authors deal with the perspective that Luke is a theologian and historian that can stand on his own two feet. They argue that although Luke was undoubtedly affected by being a companion of Paul, his writing predates Paul's epistles and seem to have a different intent and perspective. If Luke is allowed to speak for himself and is **not** read through Pauline eyes and filters, it will be seen that Luke's view of the Holy Spirit may be different, though not contradictory, to Paul's view. With further study it can be seen that the views of Luke and Paul are complementary.

Two other excellent books give credence to this perspective: *Luke: Historian and Theologian*, by I. Howard Marshall and *The Charismatic Theology of St. Luke*, written by Roger Strondstad.

On the other hand, conservative Evangelicals have intellectualized the power of God and done away with many spiritual manifestations. The Aristotelian logic that has been superimposed upon biblical texts has impacted many of the conservative Evangelicals to the point of theologizing God to death. The American, Greek influenced tendency to lift the intellect above the emotions does not accurately represent the Hebrew mindset in which the Bible is written.

Hollenwegger wrote in his book *Pentecostalism*, "Now it is unquestionable that Aristotle made a great discovery. He said that if of two propositions one is the exact contradiction of the other, one must be wrong. The trouble with that logic is that it is foreign to the biblical testimony. In the Bible, God can repent, He can change His opinion, for example in the book of Jonah. He can say: 'Only forty days and Nineveh is destroyed,' and then decide not to destroy it, much to the chagrin of Jonah. God is—like a partner in marriage—not without contradiction, but totally reliable. He is not reliable like a computer, he is reliable like—well—like only Himself."[45] I believe God is unchangeable in character, but unsearchable in His judgments and unfathomable in His ways (cf. Romans 11:33).

The early Church in Acts, which undoubtedly operated as the Church was meant to operate, had openness to the Spirit and teaching. They had manifestations of the Spirit and Charismatic doctrine. New Testament Christianity, according to Acts 2, 8, 10, and 19 is the experience of receiving the gift of the Holy Spirit on

---

[45] Walter J. Hollenweger, *Pentecostalism: Origins And Developments Worldwide*, Peabody, Massachusetts, 1997, 195.

the basis of the gift of saving faith, and yet there was also developing doctrine.

After the miraculous manifestations in the first part of the Acts 2, we read in:

> And they were continually devoting themselves to the apostles' teaching and to fellowship, to the breaking of bread and to prayer.
>
> (Acts 2:42)

The Church was devoting itself to the apostle's teaching or doctrine. It was probably an oral theology that was developing, but it was a theology. The propositional, systematizing of theology would come much later.

I believe that we need a biblical balance between the Classical Pentecostal and the conservative Evangelical perspectives. There needs to be a balance between and an integration of experience with theology and oral theology with propositional, systematic theology. Genuine spiritual experience needs to be grounded in and interpreted through our biblical theology, and our biblical theology needs to be lived out in our experience. D. A. Carson says that, "Throughout history there have been pendulum swings of various sorts. The Church, unfortunately, is not exempt. At times there are enormous pressures to intellectualize and formulate the Gospel; at others, enormous pressures to 'feel' one's religious faith and develop passion for God—profound, emotional outbursts of contrition, praise, adoration.

At most times in history, of course, groups espousing each of these polarities co-exist, one perhaps on the decline, the other on the ascendancy; and most groups embrace some mixture of the two, without much thought as to their proportion. Only rarely have Christians, such as the early English Puritans, self-consciously committed themselves to wholistic integration of the two. Noncharismatic Evangelicals *tend* to the former stereotype; Charismatics (*and certainly Pentecostals*) *tend* toward the latter. Both have their dangers."[46] Of course, I believe D. A. Carson is using the term Charismatic in a similar way that we are using the term Pentecostal.

We are seeking to do what Carson sees Christians as rarely doing. We are seeking to establish a group of Christians who are committed to the wholistic integration of these two perspectives, i.e. we seek to contemplate and formulate the Gospel, while experiencing and feeling our faith in legitimate biblical experience!

Allow me to sketch the historical backdrop of this discussion. In reading Donald Dayton's *Theological Roots Of Pentecostalism*, I became aware of the fact that the climate and religious developments of the mid-1800's to 1900, just before the modern Pentecostal movement began, are very important to understanding present theological developments.

It was interesting for me to see that the Wesleyan Holiness Movement during that time, eventually evolved

[46] D. A. Carson, *Showing the Spirit*, Baker Books, Grand Rapids, Michigan, 1987, 106.

into two prominent movements: a movement that touted a second work of grace or blessing of "entire sanctification or holiness" and the Pentecostal teaching of the baptism with the Holy Spirit bringing both power for service and holiness.

Just before the turn of the century, many of the prominent religious leaders of America were writing about and teaching on the baptism with the Holy Spirit. Men like Moody, Torrey, A. B. Simpson, and A. J. Gordon, were teaching that there was a baptism with the Holy Spirit available for Christians, although Moody tended to keep his experience and teaching more private and Torrey later violently denounced the Modern Pentecostal Movement. Donald Dayton says, ". . . by the mid-1890s almost every brand of the Holiness and 'higher life' movements of the nineteenth century, as well as the revivalism of the period in general, was teaching a variation of some sort or another on the baptism with the Holy Spirit, though with some significant differences in nuance and meaning.

It is thus no accident that Pentecostalism emerged when it did. All that was needed was the spark that would ignite this volatile tinder."[47]

Then we come to the controversy over who is the father of the Modern Pentecostal Movement. Some believe it is Charles Parham, at the turn of the century, while others claim William Seymour with the start of the Azuza Street

---

[47] Donald W. Dayton, *Theological Roots of Pentecostalism*, Scarecrow Press, Metuchen, New Jersey, 1987, 108.

Revival. This is important because of the nature and hermeneutic of the two movements. The nature of Parham's experience and hermeneutic was racist and puts forth the teaching of tongues being the 'initial evidence' of the baptism with the Holy Spirit. His contribution to Pentecostalism is significant. Nevertheless, I claim that William Seymour is the father of the Modern Pentecostal Movement. This is backed up by the fact that virtually every Pentecostal group in the world can trace their heritage back to the Azuza Street Revival. Furthermore, it is this theology and hermeneutic which has impacted our theology and hermeneutic. More specifically, the experience, theology, and hermeneutic of William Seymour is less radical, more biblical, and still has the potential for ongoing impact upon the world.

Walter Hollenweger said, "For if this movement be of the Spirit—which I believe with all my soul—then it is also of the Spirit that:

- It began with a black ecumenist, in the black, oral Afro-American culture, with all that implies;
- It integrated important elements of Catholic (*universal*) spirituality;
- It was inspired by the social and political interpretation of holiness developed in the American Holiness Movement;
- It developed—from its very beginning—critical elements in relation to dispensationalism, inspiration of Scripture, hermeneutics, social and political issues, and modern theological scholarship;

- It began as an ecumenical renewal movement."[48]

We still cannot understand some of the present climate within Christendom, without understanding Fundamentalism. "Fundamentalism and Pentecostalism were unrelated reactions to the state of religion at the close of the 1900s, but these unrelated movements soon began to react to each other . . . Fundamentalism was a movement back to the fundamentals of the Word of God. It was an intellectual reaction to the church of that time. It proposed a cognitive rescue of the church from its weariness. Pentecostalism was a reaction to intellectual enterprise. The Pentecostal critique focused **not** so much on diluted theology as upon withered piety. The problem, to Pentecostals, lay **not** in wrong thinking so much as in collapsed feeling. Not the decline of orthodoxy, but the decay of devotion lay at the root of the problem. It was not that the church was *liberal*, but that it was *lifeless*. *What was needed was not a new argument for heads, but a new experience for hearts.*

Fundamentalists and the neo-orthodox mounted arguments. Pentecostals gave testimony."[49] Classical Pentecostals subscribed to an oral theology, while conservative Evangelicals subscribed to a systematic, propositional theology. I was raised in the Classical Pentecostalism of "The

---

[48] Donald W. Dayton, *Theological Roots of Pentecostalism*, Scarecrow Press, Metuchen, New Jersey, 1987, 397.

[49] Walter J. Hollenweger, *Pentecostalism*, Hendrickson Publishers, Peabody, Massachusetts, 1997, 190–191, quoting Russ Spittler's, "Fundamentalists," A paper presented at an international conference at the University of Calgary, Canada, 103–116.

Church of God In Christ," but in reaction to what I considered to be excesses and abuses, I studied and taught conservative Evangelicalism in our church from 1974 to 1997. In 1997, I began a biblical reevaluation of my teaching that continues to this day. I now believe I am coming to a more moderate, biblical position.

"Pentecostalism and Fundamentalism were separate and often hostile movements, and **Pentecostalism became one of the targets of Fundamentalism**. Fundamentalists were particularly critical of Pentecostalism. It is held that the famous G. Campbell Morgan, one of the contributors to *The Fundamentals*, spoke of the Pentecostal movement as 'the last vomit of Satan.'"[50] This becomes even more important, when you understand that conservative Evangelicalism is a milder form of Fundamentalism.

Although we disagree with certain Evangelical perspectives, Evangelicals have given us a necessary propositional perspective of Christianity. Their perspective has influenced all of Christianity to seek to formulate accurate statements and propositions concerning the Word of God. On the other hand, while there are a number of things that we disagree with in the Modern Pentecostal Movement, it is important to note that we see God working through the Modern Pentecostal Movement to con-

---

[50] Walter J. Hollenweger, *Pentecostalism*, Hendrickson Publishers, Peabody, Massachusetts, 1997, 190–191, quoting Russ Spittler's, "Fundamentalists," A paper presented at an international conference at the University of Calgary, Canada, 103–116.

tinue the Reformation. The first Reformation restored the Word of God and the doctrine of justification by faith to the people. The second Reformation continues to restore to the people of the Church the power of the early Church through the manifestations of the Spirit.

The third Reformation is restoring the gifted people of Ephesians 4, i.e. ascension gifts or five fold ministerers to the church, for the equipping of the Saints.

WHAT BIBLECOSTALS™ BELIEVE

On the basis of the aforementioned understanding and history, I now sketch what it is that we believe.

We accept the Evangelical belief and those who hold the belief that the baptism in the Holy Spirit or empowering work of the Holy Spirit may occur at salvation. If one holds to this belief, we would simply urge that person to seek the filling of the Holy Spirit that Paul talks about in Ephesians 5:18.

Nevertheless, we lean towards the doctrine of subsequence (*at least logically, if not chronologically*[51]) of the empowering work of the Holy Spirit. The empowering work of the Holy Spirit is an event and an experience that is subsequent to or after salvation and is for power for believers to be witnesses of Jesus Christ, and to transact

---

[51] William and Robert Menzies, Spirit and Power: Foundations of Pentecostal Experience, Zondervan Publishing House, Grand Rapids, Michigan, 2000, 48.

Kingdom business. In the New Testament, each experience of the empowering of the Holy Spirit is accompanied by inspired speech, i.e. tongues, prophecy, and preaching with power, and that inspired speech tends to be tongues and/or prophecy. I do not teach that any of this is evidentiary, because I have no command that says, "You must have inspired speech, or tongues, or prophecy to receive the empowering ministry of the Holy Spirit." Nevertheless, from the text of Luke-Acts, I have drawn the conclusion that we should expect some kind of inspired speech, when we are "empowered by the Holy Spirit" for service.

The empowering work of the Holy Spirit is known by many New Testament synonyms, but these synonyms are **dynamic** synonyms that highlight different parts of the same event. When you consider verses like Luke 24:49 and Acts 1:4, 8, the experience is to be expected and is seen as necessary to carrying out the mission of the Church. The baptism in the Spirit is sovereignly given, but there are some things that we can do to put ourselves in a position and condition to receive what God has given.

We believe that the "filling" that Paul is describing, in Ephesians 5:18, is something that every Spirit-indwelled believer should seek, and is not the baptism in the Holy Spirit that Luke describes in Acts—but the control of the Holy Spirit.

We believe the manifestations of the Spirit in 1 Corinthians 12:8–10 are still in operation.

We believe that part of the confusion over the operation of the Spirit in the New Testament proceeds from the many things that happen on the Great Day of Pentecost. On the Great Day of Pentecost, believers were probably born of the Spirit, baptized into the body of Christ through the Holy Spirit (*which signals the birthday of the Church*), indwelled by the Spirit, sealed by the Spirit for the day of redemption, baptized in the Spirit by Jesus Christ or empowered by the Spirit, possibly convicted by the Holy Spirit—this may occur just prior to salvation—, etc.

ARTICLE 1: THE DIFFERENCE BETWEEN THE BAPTISM IN THE HOLY SPIRIT AND THE FILLING WITH THE HOLY SPIRIT.

The baptism in the Holy Spirit is a baptism through the instrumentality of Jesus in the sphere of the Holy Spirit for power to carry out the mission of the Church (Luke 3:16; Acts 1:5). Because the sphere of the baptism in the Holy Spirit may also be indicated in the Greek preposition *en*, I like the phraseology "the baptism 'in' the Holy Spirit."

After studying the major passages of Acts, which have to do with the baptism in the Holy Spirit, I am making the observation that Luke uses *dynamic* synonyms when discussing the baptism in the Holy Spirit. All of these terms that are being used are dynamic synonyms for the same thing:

- Being clothed with power from on high;
- The promise of the Father;
- The baptism in the Holy Spirit;
- Receives the gift of the Holy Spirit;
- The coming of the Holy Spirit upon people;
- The filling of the Holy Spirit;
- The pouring forth of the Holy Spirit;
- The promise of the Spirit;
- The gift of the Holy Spirit;
- The falling of the Holy Spirit upon people; and
- The gift of the Holy Spirit being poured out on people.

I would add a footnote that the filling of the Holy Spirit seems to be used more than the other synonyms. I believe this is intentional and instructive. The "Lukan" filling with the Holy Spirit refers more to what was received than to what God gave. God poured out His Spirit and baptized the 120 in His Spirit. They received or were filled with the Spirit, i.e. the "Lukan" filling with the Holy Spirit. What we see here may be cause and effect! God was the cause and He intended for the effect to be the "Lukan" filling of the Holy Spirit. This effect, i.e. the effect of being filled with the Holy Spirit, I believe was supposed to be the repeatable experience of the Christian. This effect was for power for witnessing and transacting Kingdom business to carry out the mission of the Church, which includes inspired speech, and is not to be confused with Paul's "filling" of the Spirit, which is the "control" of the Holy Spirit for everyday living.

Unfortunately, for us, God has left us, not as a result of any lack of power on His behalf but because of His divine sovereignty, some choice in the matter. The giving of a gift and the receiving of a gift are two different ends of a transaction. *I can give you a gift, but whether you receive that gift and how you receive that gift is up to you.* Even though God gave the gift of the Holy Spirit to groups, in the book of Acts, the individual responses to the outpouring of the Holy Spirit were unique. *Perhaps, not everyone was filled to the same extent. Nevertheless, God intended for the normal life of the believer to be Spirit-filled or empowered to be witnesses, but alas that is not the case.*

We can accept the conservative Evangelical position that the baptism in the Holy Spirit, which occurred in Acts 2, is normative for all believers today. We can accept the view that the baptism in the Holy Spirit that Luke discusses and the baptism into the body of Christ that Paul discusses in 1 Corinthians 12:13 are the same. We can accept the view that the filling of the Spirit in Acts 2:4 and the filling of the Spirit that Paul commands in Ephesians 5:18 are the same. If Evangelicals maintain that they are baptized and filled with the Holy Spirit upon salvation, then the filling must be maintained or regained when lost through sin or the erosion of life. The danger of lifelessness is addressed in the filling of the Holy Spirit.

On the other hand, although we can accept the Evangelical position with respect to the nature and timing of the baptism in the Holy Spirit, we hold another position concerning the timing and impact of this baptism. *The position is: the baptism in the Holy Spirit is an event and an experience that is subsequent to salvation, and "the filling" talked about in Acts and "the filling" talked about in Ephesians 5:18 are not the same.* The baptism in the Holy Spirit is a vivid, concrete experience. When I use the term "experience," I mean "not mere feelings, although they are a real part of experience, but an effect that transforms and empowers lives."[52] Furthermore, the experience was not just internal, but external. Peter, in Acts 2:33, equated the promise of the Holy Spirit with God pouring forth that which they both saw and heard!!!

Evangelicals make the case that the Baptism in the Holy Spirit came upon saved people in Acts 2, because of the new dispensation, but came upon people at salvation from that point forward. An equally convincing biblical argument can be made that these people were saved in Acts 2, 8, 10, and 19 and the fact that the baptism in the Holy Spirit came subsequent to salvation seems to be normative. *(See my paper "The Baptism in the Holy Spirit/Ghost.)*

---

[52] Kilian McDonnell & George T. Montague, *Christian Initiation and Baptism in the Holy Spirit*, The Liturgical Press, Collegeville, Minnesota, 1991, 358.

This seems to be specifically stated in Acts 2:38. After Peter had preached the message of the kingdom to the gathered crowd, Luke writes:

> And Peter said to them, "Repent, and let each of you be baptized in the name of Jesus Christ for the forgiveness of your sins; and you shall receive the gift of the Holy Spirit."
>
> (Acts 2:38)

Here we see a model, if not a formula for the baptism in the Holy Spirit, which is represented by the synonymous term "the gift of the Holy Spirit." Repentance plus water baptism bring about the gift of the Holy Spirit. The internal plus the external, i.e. conversion plus the adult rite of initiation—which is water baptism—bring about the gift of the Holy Spirit, i.e. the baptism in or empowering work of the Holy Spirit. Keep in mind that neither repentance nor water baptism are meritorious. Repentance is the flip side of faith and a gift from God. Water baptism is the necessary expression of repentance and faith and a part of the biblical, conversion-initiation motif.

Furthermore, the six references to the baptism in the Holy Spirit (Matthew 3:11; Mark 1:8; Luke 3:16; John 1:33; Acts 1:5; Acts 11:16) seem to refer to a subsequent experience available to all believers. Although 1 Corinthians 12:13 can be applied to Pentecost in a way that equates the baptism in the Holy Spirit with salvation, I believe Paul is describing the unity that was created by the Baptism in the Holy Spirit, on the Great Day of Pentecost, among the already saved believers. I don't believe Paul is defining the baptism in the Holy Spirit that occurred in Acts 2, although that is when this unity was first inaugurated.

Furthermore, when we let the same author, using the same words, speak for himself, I don't believe that the "filling" of the Holy Spirit in Acts and the "filling" that Paul commands in Ephesians 5:18 are the same. In Acts, Luke is describing an event subsequent to salvation for power to be a witness and that creates the missionary community of the Church. In Ephesians, Paul is describing something that every believer should seek, i.e. the control of the indwelling Holy Spirit in every area of his/her life. The ongoing, everyday control of the Holy Spirit in a believer's life and the event and experience that empowers a believer to be a witness and transact Kingdom business are two different things.

It has been stated that nowhere does the Bible exhort us to seek the baptism in the Holy Spirit or any of the other dynamic terms. On the surface, this may seem to be true, but it will be seen to be false with a little examination.

The exhortation to seek the baptism in the Holy Spirit is stated in Luke's recounting of the familiar "Ask, Seek, and Knock" passage, in Luke 11. He summarizes this teaching differently than Matthew. He records the words of Jesus:

> If you then, being evil, know how to give good gifts to your children, how much more will your heavenly Father give the Holy Spirit to those who ask Him?
>
> (Luke 11:13)

What is Luke talking about? The length and nature of this paper will not allow a full exegesis, but Luke's intent seems to be to constantly point forward to the baptism in the Holy Spirit, on The Great Day of Pentecost. So, now, after The Great Day of Pentecost, we should ask, seek, and knock for the baptism in the Holy Spirit.

With a little study, it will also be seen that Jesus commanded His disciples to be empowered by the Holy Spirit when He told them to go to Jerusalem and wait until they were clothed with power from on high (cf. Luke 24:49; Acts 1:4). The phrase "clothed with power from on high" is another synonym for the baptism in the Holy Spirit. This is a command that captures the indispensability of the empowering of the Holy Spirit, i.e. for service.

From an Evangelical perspective, there is only one initial baptism in the Holy Spirit, but many fillings. Jesus gave the Baptism of the Holy Spirit, on the Great Day of Pentecost, and what the 120 received and experienced was the filling of the Holy Spirit. The result of the baptism with the Holy Spirit was the filling of the Holy Spirit.

According to this perspective, there is only one baptism with the Spirit, and we are exhorted to constantly seek and appropriate the filling of the Holy Spirit—

because the filling of the Holy Spirit can be lost through **sin** and the **erosion of life**. John R. Stott said, "When we speak of the baptism of the Spirit we are referring to a once-for-all gift; when we speak of the fullness of the Spirit we are acknowledging that this gift needs to be *continuously and increasingly appropriated*."[53]

From the Biblecostal™ perspective, we believe in many baptisms and many fillings. According to Acts 4:23–31, the fact that the Holy Spirit filled the disciples once, in Acts 2:4, does not preclude later fillings as in Acts 4:31.[54] If these terms are synonyms for the same experience, then what happened in Acts 4:31 can be considered another baptism. In addition, if the experience of the baptism in the Holy Spirit is for power to be a witness, would we not need fresh power in our various opportunities to witness?

In addition, as we have previously noted, Luke also wrote in Luke 11:13 that the heavenly Father would give the Holy Spirit to those who ask in prayer. It is possible that after the initial baptism in the Holy Spirit, on the Great Day of Pentecost, prayer for a fresh baptism in the

---

[53] John R. W. Stott, *Baptism & Fullness*, InterVarsity Press, Downers Grove, Illinois, 1964, 47.

[54] Kilian McDonnell & George T. Montague, *Christian Initiation and Baptism in the Holy Spirit*, The Liturgical Press, Collegeville, Minnesota, 1991, 40.

Holy Spirit, filling of the Holy Spirit, or the outpouring of the Holy Spirit is wholly appropriate.[55]

Furthermore, Paul's exhortation to be filled with the Spirit, in Ephesians 5:18, means that we should constantly seek to be filled or controlled by the Holy Spirit in our daily lives.

I do not believe that the Bible teaches that the baptism in the Holy Spirit is necessary for salvation. On the other hand, neither does it teach the present complacency with the gift of salvation, but an expectation for "Pentecostal" power for mission.

ARTICLE 2: TONGUES

There is **no** clear statement in the Bible that the spiritual manifestation of tongues, or any of the other manifestations in 1 Corinthians 12:8–10 have ceased, but there are a number of Scriptures that indicate that tongues shall continue to the end of age. Let me give you just one:

> Peter said to them, "Repent, and each of you be baptized in the name of Jesus Christ for the forgiveness of your sins; and you will receive the gift of the Holy Spirit. For the promise is for you and your children

---

[55] Kilian McDonnell & George T. Montague, *Christian Initiation and Baptism in the Holy Spirit*, The Liturgical Press, Collegeville, Minnesota, 1991, 41.

and for all who are far off, as many as the Lord our
God will call to Himself."

(Acts 2:38–39)

Now, what promise is Peter talking about? He has
already told us:

Therefore having been exalted to the right hand of
God, and having received from the Father the promise of the Holy Spirit, He has poured forth this which
you both see and hear.

(Acts 2:33)

The promise of the Holy Spirit, which was the promise
of the Father, which was also the promise to Abraham, was
poured forth with the *visible manifestation* of split tongues
of fire and the *audible manifestation* of a noise like a violent, rushing wind, and people speaking languages they
did not know, through the power of the Holy Spirit!

I prefer to use the biblical term that Paul uses in 1
Corinthians 12, *phanerosis*, or "manifestation." I do not
like the term "sign," because it seems to influence
people to seek for proof of an experience and to seek
for something other than the baptism in the Holy Spirit.
Some extraordinary manifestations occurred on the
Great Day of Pentecost, because the Great Day of Pentecost was also the inauguration of a whole new dispensation of the Holy Ghost.

The visible tongues and sound of a violent, rushing wind do not occur again, because the Holy Spirit came to earth once-and-for-all in this dispensational way. Yet, tongues and prophecy—in addition, the other manifestations of 1 Corinthians 12 that were given to each believer for the common good of the church—continue to be manifest in conjunction with the baptism in the Holy Spirit, because of the Spirit's advent to other people groups and the normative side of the event.

After much study, consideration, and reconsideration, I believe the manifestation of tongues in Acts is speaking in known, human languages that were **not** learned, through the power of the Holy Spirit, at the coming of the Holy Spirit to different people groups in keeping with Acts 1:8.

It seems that once this function was fulfilled, the nature of tongues changed. The transition may have been underway in Acts 19:1–7, because there is no statement of understanding, interpretation, or explanation of the tongues that occurred there. The nature of tongues in 1 Corinthians seems to be either a message of prophecy for the assembly, which is always to be interpreted or explained (1 Corinthians 14:5, 27, 28; Acts 2:14–21), or private language for prayer, praise, worship, and spiritual warfare (1 Corinthians 13:1; 14:2, 14), which does not necessarily need to be interpreted when spoken to God in a vault or upward towards heaven, i.e. not spoken to the assembly.

The tongues in 1 Corinthians are transrational,[56] pre-cognitive, or preconceptual language. The prefix "trans" means beyond. These post-Acts tongues are not "irrational," but "transrational," i.e. they are beyond the rational, beyond the mind. The Spirit is a higher faculty for communicating with God than the mind!

Preconceptual or precognitive language is language that is spoken directly to God. No one understands the actual syllables, but in his/her spirit the person is speaking mysteries. This person's mouth is allowed to speak out of the depth of his/her spirit, through the impetus of the Holy Spirit, before the mind conceives or conceptualizes the ideas or words. When the language is used in a private setting, it does not need interpretation. The language is not understood, not because it is not a real language, but because it is not a known conceptual language—i.e. not a language that is composed of syllables or words that represent known or familiar concepts. Preconceptual or precognitive speech is "not filtered through the mind for orderly arrangement, and which when delivered, may sound like language but is really lacking any form, syntax or specific vocabulary. It is not ecstatic, although emotion may or may not be experienced during the speaking of tongues.

The mind is functioning, although it is not leading the process. The speaker knows what he or she is doing, but may not know the meaning of what is being said."[57]

---

[56] *Spirit-Filled Life Bible* (Nashville, TN: Thomas Nelson Publishers, 1991), 1737.

[57] George Mallone, *Those Controversial Gifts*, InterVarsity, Downers Grove, Illinois, 1983, 84.

We do not believe that one has to speak in tongues to be empowered by the Holy Spirit. There is **no** statement in the Bible that tongues is the "initial evidence" of the baptism with the Holy Spirit and the historical narratives of the book of Acts do not prove this conclusively. Therefore, if someone says that s/he is empowered by the Spirit, without speaking in tongues, we accept that person's testimony.

Of course, it goes without saying, that one can be "filled" with the Spirit, from Paul's perspective, without speaking in tongues. Remember, I don't believe Paul's filling is the same as Luke's filling.

We can state, on the basis of the history of Luke-Acts, that each occurrence of the baptism in the Holy Spirit is accompanied by inspired speech (*i.e. tongues, prophecy, or preaching with power*), and that inspired speech tended to be either tongues and/or prophecy.

This manifestation may flash forth either at the initial baptism or a subsequent fresh baptism. In addition, we believe the Spirit may flash forth in any of the nine manifestations of 1 Corinthians 12:8–10, for the edification of the body of Christ.

Neither tongues nor any other manifestation of the Spirit is an end all. The manifestation of tongues does not make anyone instantly mature or sinless. All believers must still grow in the knowledge and grace of our Lord and Savior, Jesus Christ. And the manifestations can be expressed in an immature or fleshly way.

Furthermore, we do **not** teach nor tolerate an attitude of "the haves" and the "have nots." We do not believe that those who speak in tongues are automatically more spiritual than those who have not spoken in tongues, because tongues are a non-mentorious gift.

ARTICLE 3: THE MANIFESTATION OF THE SPIRIT

I see **no** Bible text that states that the manifestation of the Spirit, which is delineated in nine ways in 1 Corinthians 12, has ceased. Those who maintain that the phrase "the perfect," in 1 Corinthians 13:10, refers to the canon of the Bible, do so with arguments from silence—because that is not the context of the passage and nothing concerning this is directly stated in the passage.

Most scholars, believe the phrase "the perfect," in the NASB or "that which is perfect," in the KJV, refers to the Second Coming of Jesus, the Christ.

Therefore, I affirm that the manifestation of the Spirit that is seen in nine ways is still in operation today and available to every believer. Additional reasons are as follows:

1) The Bible says as much in 1 Corinthians 14:26.
2) Peter's quoting of Joel 2:28–32, in Acts 2:17–21, highlights the fact that God was pouring out His Spirit upon all mankind or flesh.
3) Peter clearly states, in Acts 2:39, that the promise of the gift of the Holy Spirit is for you, your children, all who are afar off, and as many as the Lord shall call.

4) The imagery of the Red Sea relating to salvation and the Jordan River relating to the advent of the Holy Spirit in Acts (Exodus 14; Joshua 3).

5) The fact that God is the same, yesterday, today, and forever (Heb. 13:8).

We further affirm that while the Spirit may repeatedly use certain believers in certain manifestations, these manifestations are not the exclusive possession of any one believer, but are given to all believers, as the Spirit wills, and they flash forth for the edification of the body of Christ (1 Corinthians 12:7). This does not preclude the Holy Spirit from repeatedly giving a particular manifestation to certain individual believers or God giving gifted individuals to the church (Ephesians 4:11).

ARTICLE 4: THE BAPTISM IN THE HOLY SPIRIT AND SANCTIFICATION

We believe that the believer is born of the Spirit (John 3:6), sanctified positionally, at salvation, from the penalty of sin and in his/her spiritual walk is being progressively sanctified through the power of the indwelling Holy Spirit, and will one day be sanctified, ultimately or finally, from the presence of sin. The baptism in the Holy Spirit, who is the Spirit of sanctification, which brings power for witnessing and service, is a part of ongoing sanctification. We do not hold to a second work or blessing of grace that grants the believer entire sanctification. We do believe that a fresh baptism in the Holy Spirit will afford the believer new power to be a witness to Jesus, the Christ, which will have some impact upon the believer's ongoing sanctification or holiness.

ARTICLE 5: THE HOLY SPIRIT AND GIFTS OF HEALINGS

We do believe that God gives "gifts of healings." We do not believe that God gives a permanent gift of healing that can be manipulated by the right amount of faith, although faith may sometimes be the critical element in a specific healing. We believe that the Holy Spirit gives "gifts of healings" according to the sovereignty of God. This does not preclude the Holy Spirit from using a believer repeatedly in a particular ministry of healing.

This is the continuing development of Biblecostal™ theology and hermeneutic. If this seems too close to Classical Pentecostalism at times and very much like conservative Evangelicalism at other times, it is because we are trying to put forth a balanced biblical perspective. It is a quest for the "radical middle."[58] Kilian McDonnell said that Pentecostalism is: "Those Christians who stress the power and presence of the Holy Spirit and the Gifts of the

---

[58] Bill Jackson, *The Quest for the Radical Middle*, Vineyard International Publishing, CapeTown, South Africa, 1999, Jacket Cover.

Spirit directed toward the proclamation that Jesus Christ is Lord to the glory of God the Father."[59] This sounds like a "Word and power" or "Word and Spirit" church. This definition is very similar to what God is giving to me at this time; i.e. to teach and facilitate an encounter and experience with God and His power that is based upon the Word of God!

---

[59] McDonnell (with Bittlinger), *Problem*, quoted by Villafane, *The Liberating Spirit*, 85, and Synan, "Pentecostalism," 32.

To order additional copies of

The Eight Ministries of the HOLY SPIRIT

Have your credit card ready and call

Toll free: (877) 421-READ (7323)

or send $12.99* each plus $5.95 S&H** to

WinePress Publishing
PO Box 428
Enumclaw, WA 98022

or order online at: www.winepresspub.com

*Washington residents, add 8.4% sales tax

**add $1.00 S&H for each additional book ordered